ONE FAITH

THE EVANGELICAL CONSENSUS

J. I. PACKER AND
THOMAS C. ODEN

InterVarsity Press
Downers Grove, Illinois

InterVarsity Press
P.O. Box 1400, Downers Grove, IL 60515-1426
World Wide Web: www.ivpress.com
E-mail: mail@ivpress.com

InterVarsity Press® is the book-publishing division of InterVarsity Christian Fellowship/USA®, a student movement active on campus at hundreds of universities, colleges and schools of nursing in the United States of America, and a member movement of the International Fellowship of Evangelical Students. For information about local and regional activities, write Public Relations Dept., InterVarsity Christian Fellowship/USA, 6400 Schroeder Rd., P.O. Box 7895, Madison, WI 53707-7895, or visit the IVCF website at <www.intervarsity.org>.

Design: Cindy Kiple

Images: Don Bishop/Getty Images

ISBN 0-8308-3239-4

Printed in the United States of America ∞

Library of Congress Cataloging-in-Publication Data

One faith: the evangelical consensus/James I. Packer and Thomas C. Oden.
p. cm.
Includes bibliographical references and index.
ISBN 0-8308-3239-4 (alk. paper)
1. Evangelicalism. 2. Theology, Doctrinal. I. Packer, J. I. (James Innell) II. Oden, Thomas C.
BR1640.O54 2004
230'.04624—dc22

2003027943

P 17 16 15 14 13 12 11 10 9 8 7 6 5 4 3 2 1
Y 16 15 14 13 12 11 10 09 08 07 06 05 04

Contents

Topical Outline

INTRODUCTION

The following pages present a series of extracts from evangelical statements of faith produced between 1950 and the present day. These texts have been selected and arranged in topical sequence. Many such documents were available to us, for few evangelical organizations and associations have failed to produce at least one. All of them, in a broad sense, have a defining intent: they are *declarative* of the sponsoring body's belief; *defensive*, more or less, against deviations; and *directional* as indicators of their producers' purposes and priorities. They embody a shared interpretation of the Bible, a shared understanding of the gospel, and a shared view of the church and its mission, and when on occasion they differ from each other in detail it is within this overall frame of agreement. Each of them is a consensus statement from and for the constituency it represents. As we hope to show, each is evidence for the generic similarity of the constituencies and, indeed, for their convergence on the things that for evangelicals are crucial. We want our readers to see the range, content and quality of the evangelical consensus as a whole, and this goal has guided us in compiling the present book.

WHAT IS MEANT BY CONSENSUS?

To make clear what we mean by *consensus*, we must refer to the composing, embracing and arranging of the material we will use.

First, *composing*. None of the statements we quote were the work of one individual in isolation. All emerged from a process of dialogue and interaction. Each one was hammered out by evangelical Christians seeking together to affirm the essence and heart of what they believed, in the face of actual or potential misbelief or, at the very least, misunderstanding. Consistently these statements exhibit the framers' dual purpose: to align themselves with what faithful Christians have always believed and to show the basis of their own corporate endeavors. Their statements thus have both a personal and a corporate significance, since they express not only the drafters' consensus among themselves as individuals but also their collective consensus with what they take to be the authentic faith of the people of God.

Second, *embracing*. Many of the statements we draw on have already secured the consent of large numbers of evangelicals, which gives them consensus status in a further sense. Consensus at this level becomes reality as individuals give free and voluntary consent to what is offered them—in this case a viable accord on points previously controverted or confused. Consent expresses harmony of opinion, sentiment and intention. To consent is to *think and feel* (Latin, *sentire*) *with* (Latin prefix, *con-*) other believers and to go along with them on the basis of being in agreement with them. Acceptance only under protest, or refusal to cooperate in practice, is not an expression of consent but a denial of it. At the root and center of today's countrywide, continent-wide and worldwide solidarity of evangelicals is consensus about what these statements formulate as the essentials of biblical Christian faith. The statements, backed as they are by creeds and confessions from past times, have been so welcomed, embraced and consented to, and the bodies sponsoring them have been so accepted, trusted and supported, that transnational, transdenominational, transcultural unity of faith among evangelicals has become a demonstrable global fact.

The widespread image of evangelicals is one of people who cannot be expected to agree, either with each other or with the rest of the church on earth: people who are famous, indeed notorious, for eccentric individualism, for fighting and splitting, for dissenting and separating. But in fact, evangelicals worldwide are today unified on all the basics, and their consensus is due in large part to their embrace of some of the documents that we cite. (We have respectfully attempted not to select passages on which evangelical consent is still under intense debate.)

It is undeniable that dissent from the established order was often the seedbed out of which evangelical faith sprouted on both sides of the Atlantic, and that might be true in the future as well. But the evangelical purpose always was, and still is, to get back to apostolic Christianity as the New Testament portrays it, and evangelicals must never lose sight of this driving concern. The statements we quote would not have been embraced did they not reflect the belief that the people of God only go forward into life-transforming, world-changing fruitfulness as they go back more faithfully to apostolic certainties and truths. This belief lies at the heart of the consensus we hope to illuminate.

This collection embraces texts from two related but distinguishable wings of modern evangelical history: the Calvinist, Lutheran and Baptist wing of the Reformation, as distinguished in tone and accent in some ways from the Arminian, Wesleyan, Holiness, Charismatic and Pentecostal wing. The former group has written far more of the confessional-type documents, but the latter has written sufficiently. Our purpose is not to hold one over against the other but to view both streams flowing into contemporary worldwide evangelical teaching, and to stress language and points that demonstrate convergence rather than divergence.

Third, *arranging*. Our aim in writing this book is more than informational; beyond this, it is devotional, catechetical, systematic and ethical. Its purpose, in a word, is to *edify:* that is, to help our readers into deeper understanding of Christian truth, richer fellowship with God on the basis of it and more faithful obedience to its demands in daily life. Thus we present the texts in a sequence designed to highlight the reality and coherence of the evangelical theological consensus, in order to make it as easy as we can for readers to see the unifying convergence that has become increasingly clear to us. Our happy, irenic task is to show from the texts themselves their similarities, congruencies and eye-to-eye vistas, both implicit and explicit, as to what evangelicals share. We decline to discuss secondary matters on which disagreements surface, such as variations of polity, modes and subjects of baptism, glossolalia, millennialism, theological epistemology, and specifics of exegesis. Our hope is that readers will not be so focused on detecting and exploring such divergences in the evangelical world as to miss the point of what we are doing. This book celebrates the work of God in bringing evangelicals together in fundamentals, and that is the reality on which we labor to keep all eyes trained.

Can the Whole Picture Be Grasped at Once?

We contend that there is a cohesive picture to be grasped here—a comprehensive foundational design for the broad-based and lofty reality of the historic Christian life of faith, as expressed on paper in theologies, liturgies and hymns, and in life by repentance, trust, thanksgiving, hope, holiness, love and fellowship with the Father and his Son, Jesus Christ, through the agency of the Holy Spirit. Evangelicals who are habitually locked in battle with other evangelicals on secondary matters of the kind listed above and persons observing evangelical Christianity from outside it may have difficulty grasping this whole picture. Respectfully we ask them to make the effort as they move through this book, and we offer an analogy to show what kind of effort is needed.

Tesserae are tiny colored stones used to form an image. They have been used to make icons on church walls and pictures on Roman pavements. Each tessera is a simple cube of pigmented hard stone or beautiful durable mineral. Variously colored, tesserae have served artists as the palette of colors serves the modern painter. When artists use tesserae, what is important is not the beauty of each little stone in isolation, striking as that might be, but its part in the beautiful whole. In the same way, each separate sentence or paragraph that we quote, however impressive in itself, is to be viewed not as standing on its own but as part of the total understanding and experience of the gospel being communicated: God with us through the incarnate life, atoning death, bodily resurrection, present reign and future return of Jesus Christ the Lord, and us with God in faith and love now and forever through Christ and the Holy Spirit.

As the tesserae have no separate or significant identity apart from the picture to which they belong, and as a dab of color on canvas means nothing apart from the picture that includes it, so the texts we cite belong to a larger picture. There are no personal names or bizarre quirks attached to them. They are simply to be read as part of the fruit of cooperative endeavor to crystallize and set in order the things God makes known to us—indeed, tells the world—in Holy Scripture, namely, the full truth about him and ourselves.

But assuming that you will look for the whole picture, will you be able to see it? Consensus in understanding God's truth is an elusive thing to discern, as is truth itself, simple though Scripture makes it. The problem is the pride, perversity and unworthy passions of our fallen and sinful hearts, qualities that are never more potent in clouding our judgment about the things of God than when we are unaware of them and are ready to deny their reality. Paul refers to persons who are always learning yet never able to arrive at a knowledge of the truth (2 Tim 3:7), a situation true of many people today. Recognition of the evangelical consensus as the biblically revealed, faithfully reproduced truth of God—awesome, beautiful, gracious, commanding—is a divine gift, an opening of the eyes of the heart, and a puncturing of pride and pretense; it is an event of doxology and illumination, avowal and acknowledgment. What is avowed? The truth of the gospel, which the consensus attests. What is acknowledged? The grace of God in and through the living Lord, Jesus Christ. From where does the illumination come? From the Holy Spirit, whose help should be sought whenever questions about the meaning of Scripture or the understanding of God's revelation come up.

The evangelical consensus was, and is, at every point a refraction of a God-given discernment of how all that is in the Bible fits together as a single Christ-centered message of grace to sinners, just as the tesserae fit together in one glorious design. This discernment of the Bible and its Christ is something that all evangelicals share (and not evangelicals alone), and all the ingredients in the evangelical consensus are part of it. The dawning of this discernment, the "ah-ha" recognition of the reality at which one has been looking but which one has hitherto not seen, comes as a gift from God. Psychologists would call it pattern acknowledgment; Christians celebrate it as the teaching of the Holy Spirit, whose special role it is to open the eyes of mind and heart. C. S. Lewis tells how, when he set off to Whipsnade Zoo in the sidecar of his brother's motorbike, he did not believe that Jesus Christ was the Son of God, yet when they arrived he found he did. So we also, by inspecting the tesserae of the evangelical consensus, may find ourselves sharing the discernment of beautiful, integrated divine truth that each affirmation helps to express. This is the kind of consensus recognition that we hope our book will help mediate.

When this recognition comes, you will not need some expert to authenticate it. You will already have the authentication within—what Scripture calls the inner witness of the Holy Spirit. It is, precisely, an undeniable, irrefutable perception of the undergirding unity of the catholic Christian faith. Further analysis will evidence and confirm in detail the historical, intellectual, metaphysical and moral coherence and authority of what you have perceived, but your certainty as of now does not wait or depend on such analysis. You know what you have seen, and no one can take that from you.

The word *catholic* (with a small *c*) as a description of Christian faith means "according to the whole" (Greek, *holos*). The biblically proper reason for applying the term to the church, or any part of it, is that the wholeness and fullness of the biblical revelation of God's truth is faithfully held within the church. Evangelicals today are becoming articulate once more about this, and that is surely a happy thing. For the witness of the Holy Spirit is integral to catholic faith, and the integrated message of the Bible is basic to catholic identity, and to Christian life in its true wholeness.

A picture is grasped and a design discerned "according to the whole" when each part is seen to belong to the artist's overall scheme and to make its own contribution to the planned end product. Claimed catholicity becomes maimed catholicity if elements of biblical teaching are overlooked. Thus people in the Eastern Orthodox tradition, who understand Scripture in terms of patristic tradition, will fault evangelicals for forgetting what they see as important parts of the whole, such as the eucharistic mystery and apostolic succession; at the same time, evangelicals may fault Orthodox practice for overlooking such key parts of the whole as intimate personal trust in Jesus or pressing on with the Great Commission. In the same way, evangelicals will censure liberal Protestants for wholesale jettisoning of Bible teaching about belief and behavior. The evangelical consensus ventures to claim catholicity as essentially an intuitive, integrated, synoptic, organic grasp of the full biblical picture of God and godliness—a picture substantively solid, unified and lovely, whatever detail work it may still seem to need. And the evangelical confidence is that anyone who engages seriously with the Bible, humbly asking God for light, will duly see what millions of Christians from the beginning have been privileged to see, namely, this great picture in all its divine glory.

What Is Meant by *Evangelical?*

Evangelical Christians, in our definition, are those who read the Bible as God's own Word, addressed personally to each of them here and now; and who live out of a personal trust in, and love for, Jesus Christ as the world's only Lord and Savior. They are people who see themselves as sinners saved by grace through faith for glory; who practice loyal obedience to God; and who are active both in grateful, hopeful communion with the triune God by prayer, and in neighbor-love, with a lively commitment to disciple-making according to the Great Commission.

Different people profile evangelicals in different ways in light of their own interests. Historians categorize evangelicals as people who emphasize (1) the Bible as the Word of God, (2) the cross as the place where salvation was won, (3) conversion as a universal need and (4) missionary outreach as a universal task. Theologians dissect evangelicalism as a compound of the classic trinitarianism of Nicaea, the Cappadocians and Augustine; the classic Christology of Chalcedon; the classic soteriology and ecclesiology of the Reformation; the classic pneumatology of the Puritans and Edwards; and the classic missiology of Carey, Venn and Hudson Taylor.

Evangelical self-descriptions are varied. One example is found in Fuller Theological Seminary's 1983 explication ("What We Believe and Teach") of their 1972 "Statement of Faith," a consensus-seeking attempt at defining *evangelical* viewed in relation to two previous historic attempts to focus the core of biblical faith:

> Not long after the great Evangelical awakenings, the Evangelical Alliance, led by Thomas Chalmers in 1846, stated its faith in a cluster of nine affirmations: 1) the inspiration of the Bible; 2) the right and duty of private judgment in the interpretation of the Scriptures; 3) the Trinity; 4) human depravity; 5) the mediation of the divine Christ; 6) justification by faith; 7) conversion and sanctification by the Holy Spirit; 8) the return of Christ and judgment; 9) the ministry of the Word. Still later, in 1910, five fundamentals were identified to distinguish Evangelicals from the liberalism that threatened the church: 1) the miracles of Christ; 2) the virgin birth of Christ; 3) the satisfaction view of the atonement; 4) the verbal inspiration of the Scriptures; and 5) the bodily resurrection of Christ. Following this Evangelical pattern, the Fuller Statement of Faith includes ten central affirmations which we 'hold to be essential' to our ministry: 1) the existence, perfection and triune nature of God; 2) the revelation of God in creation, history and in Jesus Christ; 3) the inspiration and authority of the Scriptures; 4) God's creation of the world and humankind, with humanity's rebellion and subsequent depravity; 5) the person and work of Jesus Christ, including his deity, virgin birth, true humanity, substitutionary death, bodily resurrection, and ascension to heaven; 6) the Holy Spirit's work in regeneration and justification; 7) growth in the knowledge of God and Christian obedience; 8) the church as the creation of the Holy Spirit; 9) the worship,

mission and service of the church; 10) the return of Christ to raise the dead and to judge the world.

That there is here something of an evangelical confessional pattern is confirmed when we set alongside Fuller's statement the recast doctrinal basis that InterVarsity Christian Fellowship adopted as recently as 2000.

We believe in:

The only true God, the almighty Creator of all things,
existing eternally in three persons—
Father, Son, and Holy Spirit—full of love and glory.

The unique divine inspiration,
entire trustworthiness
and authority of the Bible.

The value and dignity of all people:
created in God's image to live in love and holiness,
but alienated from God and each other because of our sin and guilt,
and justly subject to God's wrath.

Jesus Christ, fully human and fully divine,
who lived as a perfect example,
who assumed the judgment due sinners by dying in our place,
and who was bodily raised from the dead and ascended as Savior and Lord.

Justification by God's grace to all who repent
and put their faith in Jesus Christ alone for salvation.

The indwelling presence and transforming power of the Holy Spirit,
who gives to all believers a new life and a new calling to obedient service.

The unity of all believers in Jesus Christ,
manifest in worshiping and witnessing churches
making disciples throughout the world.

The victorious reign and future personal return of Jesus Christ,
who will judge all people with justice and mercy,
giving over the unrepentant to eternal condemnation
but receiving the redeemed into eternal life.

The controlling principle of inclusion in these two statements is clear from the phrase "hold to be essential." Evangelicalism identifies a core of necessary truth that has remained central through many shifts of the Christian scene over time. This core is demonstrably the content of historic Protestant-evangelical teaching and is in fact the consensual frame and glue that holds the present book together. It is the centered doctrinal foundation of what is nowadays being called not just the evangelical movement but the evangelical church. Once the parachurch movements saw themselves as auxiliary to the denominations, but as denominations recede in significance and parachurch evangelicalism grows stronger, it becomes increasingly fitting and important for evangelicalism to proclaim its transdenominational, Bible-based confessional unity in an explicit way—as statements of the kind quoted are actually doing.

Both within and outside the denominations of the Protestant establishment there has been a major evangelical resurgence since the mid-twentieth century. There has been a renewal of the evangelical mind, a fresh intellectual blossoming in exegetical, theological, historical and philosophical studies, marked by new academic institutions and societies and a remarkable flow of publications written at the highest levels of academic competence and integrity. In addition, there has been a renewal, through the charismatic movement, of what we may call the evangelical spirit, the rediscovering of the universality of spiritual gifts for service (in music, worship, pastoral care and mission) and the rebirth of biblical preaching. Numbers are not everything, but old churches have grown, new churches have been formed, and megachurches have burst forth. Evangelicals are being regenerated both in mind and heart, and their unity is deepening as they converge and cooperate in outreach.

The strength of the doctrinal consensus underlying this movement of advance is what we seek to exhibit in this book. This, we think, is the right time to attempt that. After half a century during which evangelicals have been on the march all over the world, practicing cooperative *unity in mission* in transdenominational contexts, it is well to show that, so far from being mere opportunist pragmatism, this joint action has been undergirded by *unity in faith and doctrine.*

How Have These Texts That Show the Evangelical Consensus Been Laid Out?

We have arranged our citations with minimal interference from intruding interpretations. The consensual convergences will become clear from the texts themselves.

The principle of selection has been both quantitative and qualitative—quantitative in that we looked for statements that are widely representative of international evangelical witness; qualitative in that we looked for statements that are biblically and theologically excellent.

The principle of arrangement is the ordinary and familiar sequence of the early baptismal confessions, the catholic creeds of the patristic era, and the later Reformation confessions and catechisms. The triune order that we follow (the Father—creation; the Son—redemption; the Holy Spirit—transformation) was the organizing principle of orthodox instruction from Cyril of Jerusalem to John of Damascus. It is basically the order followed from Calvin and John Pearson to W. B. Pope and Charles Hodge, and most key Protestant writers, theologians and educators today. Thus arranged, this book could serve as a text or resource for Christian teaching in many contexts. Anyone who seeks an unpretentious cohesive survey of basic biblical teaching, digested for church use, will find one here.

Our historically tested sequence of themes runs thus: Scripture, God, man, Jesus Christ, his life, death, resurrection, and return, justification by grace through faith, the holy life, the church, and the future. We focus more on doctrinal basics than on moral teachings, though the latter are implicitly interwoven throughout. We present faith statements of worldwide evangelical movements or globally significant evangelical institutions or evangelical confessions that encompass or express the transdenominational consensus of evangelical believers. Denominational statements, however robust in their evangelicalism, have been ruled out, with few exceptions, since we are trying to show a transdenominational evangelical consensus.

Under each doctrinal heading we begin with one primary selection that serves, in our view, as the fullest and fittest summary statement on the topic. These are printed in bold type. The other citations amplify what the bold-type extracts crystallize.

Is the Evangelical Consensus Ecumenically Significant?

We must tread carefully when discussing the ecumenical significance of this book. Our answer to whether the book is ecumenically significant is no and yes, and requires fairly detailed explication.

During the half-century from which our extracts come, *evangelical* and *ecumenical* were terms pointing to two very different and in some ways rival movements. So different were they that the term *ecumenical* still grinds most harshly in the ears of many evangelicals, while to many of the ecumenicists, as we may call them, *evangelical* remains a pariah word for a class of people beyond the pale. The fact is that the ecumenical movement was first engendered in the mid-nineteenth century (1846) by evangelicals, evangelists and missionaries who formed the Evangelical Alliance largely to support and strengthen Christian outreach, and at the start its basis of action was doctrinally solid. A century later, however, Protestant liberals reshaped its commitments and reinterpreted its Christian affirmations drastically, partly through politicization, partly through secularization and partly through capitulation to modern influences. By the 1966 Geneva Conference on Church and

Society this takeover was perceived as virtually irreversible, and the 1973 Bangkok Conference on Faith and Order, when mission was reconceived primarily as a socioeconomic endeavor and salvation as the fruit of that endeavor, confirmed that judgment. Meanwhile, the "mainline" Protestant bodies that maintained the World Council of Churches were increasingly sidelined in their own wider communities, while evangelical strength grew, a dual process that continues today.

By 2000 what might be called a New Ecumenism was emerging, regrounded in classic Christianity and drawing together the biblically orthodox from pre-Reformation, Reformation and post-Reformation traditions. All these efforts point a way to possible closer consolidation and cooperation, uncompromising, uncompromised and within recognized limits, between conservative Christian constituencies. Clearly any such development would have to be based on the primacy of Scripture, the truth of the Trinity, a biblical view of the uniqueness and universal claims of Christ, classic Christian sexual ethics, and a serious commitment to fulfilling the Great Commission by worldwide church-planting evangelism—all matters on which the evangelical consensus runs in tension with radical feminism, self-styled sexual liberation, culture-of-death and antifamily ideologies, nanny-state and victimization politics, moral relativism across the board, and other related aberrations of our day. Time alone will tell how potent this vision of biblically grounded Christian solidarity may prove to be.

Therefore, while the contents of this book may seem irrelevant and wrong-headed to devotees of the Old (meaning modernistic) Ecumenism, they may well serve to further the quest of the New (meaning newly discovered historic) Ecumenism for recovering authentic Christian unity and furthering concerted Christian action.

It is true that evangelical theology has often been marred by contentiousness, divisiveness and polemics that need not have been so harsh, and that its sights have usually been trained more on victory than on unity. Our citations, however, show God moving in our time to generate consensual affirmations that both express and advance evangelical unity in a way that brings us closer to other orthodox believers. This is a fact worth highlighting.

A further fact worth noting is that in the first half of the twentieth century, evangelicals, with others—though usually for different reasons—took a "supersessionist" view of the Jewish people. They held that God's new covenant with the church had replaced his former covenant with Israel and that Jewish people now had no significance in God's plan. When the facts about the Holocaust became known, however, the ways divided: liberals concluded that Christianity had so disgraced itself that evangelizing Jews was no longer possible, and that God's covenant with Abraham offered Jews salvation without Christ in any case. Evangelicals, on the other hand, were spurred by the stigma of anti-Semitism and the theology of Paul to fresh outreach endeavors to Jewish people as a matter of prime importance in this and every age—as our citations testify.

It is apparent that the writers of these evangelical faith statements were more concerned with trustworthy doctrinal content than with style. Yet as editors who value clear and concise argument in moving language, we think many of the sentences we quote are both polished and persuasive. Some are provocative; some are glorious and touching. They gain their energy from the fact that evangelicals are passionate about biblical teaching. Those who think that evangelicals are complacent and not self-critical should note how often, and how strongly, the faithful are called to repent of such things as racism, false piety and neglect of the poor, and how profoundly some bad evangelical habits are criticized.

WHAT PRACTICAL USEFULNESS MAY A BOOK LIKE THIS HAVE?

The usefulness of this book lies partly in the fact that it points evangelicals to the common language of their own recent heritage and contributes to correcting some common derogatory stereotypes. For example, when evangelicals are charged with hypocrisy, introversion and parochialism as a lifestyle, it may be apropos to quote the Manila Manifesto:

> Our message that Christ reconciles alienated people to each other rings true only if we are seen to love and forgive one another, to serve others in humility, and to reach out beyond our own community in compassionate, costly ministry to the needy. Our challenge to others to deny themselves, take up their cross and follow Christ will be plausible only if we ourselves have evidently died to selfish ambition, dishonesty and covetousness, and are living lives of simplicity, contentment and generosity.

Even if evangelicals do not always live up to their ideals, they have most certainly set high standards for themselves.

When evangelicals are said to be schismatic and unconcerned with the unity of the body of Christ, it will not be out of order to point to the Preamble to The Gospel of Jesus Christ: An Evangelical Celebration, which states: "All Christians are called to unity in love and unity in truth." Or when it is said that evangelicals are in love with division and separation, reference may be made to the DuPage Declaration:

> We deplore the scandalous isolation and separation of Christians from one another. We believe such division is contrary to Christ's explicit desire for unity among his people and impedes the witness of the church in the world.

When evangelicals are accused of demeaning women, we may call to mind the assertion of the Manila Manifesto, that

> God created men and women as equal bearers of his image, accepts them equally in Christ and poured out his Spirit on all flesh, sons and daughters alike. In addition, because the Holy Spirit distributes his gifts to women as well as to men, they must be given opportunity to exercise their gifts.

While this leaves some questions open, it calls into question the stereotypes.

When the media depict evangelicals as entrenched political conservatives constantly positioning themselves against the poor, one may note World Vision's representative desire that Jesus should be

> central in our individual and corporate lives. We seek to follow him—in his identification with the poor, the afflicted, the oppressed, the marginalized; in his special concern for children; in his respect for the dignity bestowed by God on women equally with men; in his challenge to unjust attitudes and systems; in his call to share resources with each other; in his love for all people without discrimination or conditions; in his offer of new life through faith in him.

Or when, upon exposure of specific scandals, people assume that all evangelicals are inclined to condone financial graft in ministry and easy acceptance of a consumer ethic, we can quote the Lausanne Covenant, which states that

> a church which preaches the cross must itself be marked by the cross. It becomes a stumbling block to evangelism when it betrays the gospel or lacks a living faith in God, a genuine love for people, or scrupulous honesty in all things including promotion and finance. The church is the community of God's people rather than an institution, and must not be identified with any particular culture, social or political system, or human ideology.

The foregoing are only samples (not a complete list by any means) of the "evangelical embarrassments" that critics allege. Something about evangelicalism provokes intense and sustained lampooning. But evangelical belief is no more, or no less, than faithful echoing of biblical teaching, and plain biblical Christianity is what the complainants are criticizing. We hope this book will serve to make that clear.

Over and above flip and satirical critics there are those today who genuinely want to know what enlivens evangelicals and why they are exponentially growing. It is estimated that half a billion of the world's inhabitants profess some form of evangelical faith. Approximately one out of four Christians worldwide are evangelicals, with huge and rapidly increasing numbers in the Southern Hemisphere.

From what roots does this tenacity and energy come? We hope we are helping to answer that question by laying out representative confessional statements to correct biased stereotypes.

Who Are the Intended Readers?

Who are the interested parties that we address? Pastors, students, scholars, teachers, media communicators, sociologists, journalists, Christian laypeople nurtured in nonevangelical versions of the faith, and thoughtful secularists who from time to time wonder what Christianity is really all about. Agnostics, Muslims and adherents of other world religions will, we hope, be found among fairminded inquirers at this point. Most of all, we believe that rank-and-file evangelical laity will be enriched and encouraged by seeing their heritage thus laid out before them in a broad-based and persuasive way.

Although this book is initially designed for straight-through reading by evangelical laypeople, it can also serve as a reference work on key documents of evangelical faith. Admittedly our primary audience is Christian laypersons and serious readers of Scripture who are aware of the growing power and intellectual plausibility of evangelical teaching but who desire to see its emerging unity spelled out more deliberately and expressed textually. But many nonevangelical people remain truly curious about what makes evangelicals tick. In and by this book we invite critics and inquirers to examine the beliefs evangelicals think most crucial to their faith.

In addition to lay readers, we hope, as we indicated above, that these texts will be useful for the following professionals:

- pastors and church leaders preaching or teaching on basic Christian doctrine or doctrines (creation, the cross, grace, the future—a goldmine for preaching is waiting in these sections)
- students in courses on basic Christian doctrine, missiology, evangel-

ism and modern church history at churches, colleges and seminaries

- historians, theologians, ecumenists and sociologists who have never been accurately introduced to evangelical teaching
- journalists, librarians and teachers who are in need of a standard reference work on evangelicalism

What Are the Sources?

Earlier collections of confessional documents have often been presented as the creedal heritage of geographically or denominationally organized families of churches. Such are Philip Schaff, *The Creeds of Christendom* (latest printing, Grand Rapids: Baker, 1985), which ends with the First World Conference on Faith and Order at Lausanne, 1927; Mark A. Noll, *Confessions and Catechisms of the Reformation* (Grand Rapids: Baker, 1991), which ends with the thirty-nine Articles of the Church of England, 1571; John Leith, *Creeds of the Churches* (Atlanta: John Knox Press, 1982), the third edition of which ends with the Assembly of the World Council of Churches at Nairobi, 1975; James Benjamin Green, *A Harmony of the Westminster Presbyterian Standards* (Richmond: John Knox Press, 1951), which includes texts only from the Reformed tradition; and Thomas C. Oden, *Doctrinal Standards in the Wesleyan Tradition* (Grand Rapids: Zondervan, 1988), which is limited in a similar way.

By contrast, the documents that follow come almost entirely from transdenominational, parachurch and cross-traditional sources, which puts them in a different category from church confessions. The bodies and gatherings that produced them included evangelicals from all the Reformational and post-Reformation church families that have been growing during the past fifty years, and this has given them an ecumenical, unitive, Bible-based, rallying call and character that is distinctively theirs. All of them have the practical purposes of evangelism, nurture, and maturation and invigoration of fellowships and congregations clearly and constantly in view. All of them intend to speak of and for real ministry to real people. All of them center, one way or another, on affirming, confirming, clarifying, celebrating and applying the revealed truth of the gospel of Jesus Christ. In this connection we commend John Stott's volume *Making Christ Known* (Grand Rapids: Eerdmans, 1996), a collection of Historic Mission Documents from the Lausanne Movement, 1974-89. That compilation is focused more on mission than doctrine and is chronologically arranged, whereas our collection is systematically arranged with a steady doctrinal-confessional focus.

One person stands out as the human catalyst for the production of these materials: Dr. Billy Graham. While he neither invented the form nor drafted the texts themselves, it was he who initiated the consultative and networking gatherings on world evangelism out of which statements of prime and pioneering significance emerged. Following the Berlin Congress of 1966, the International Congress on World Evangelism met at Lausanne in 1974, where representatives of 150 nations approved and embraced the seminal Lausanne Covenant. The fifteen-point Amsterdam Affirmations were developed at the International Conference for Itinerant Evangelists, attended by over four thousand, in 1983, and in 1989 participants in the Second International Congress on World Evangelization explicated the Lausanne Covenant as the Manila Manifesto. Climactically, more than ten thousand church leaders, theologians and mission strategists from more than two hundred countries came together in 2000, again in Amsterdam, and gave the world the Amsterdam Declaration as "a charter for evangelism in the 21st century": "Evangelicals come from many churches, languages and cultures but we hold in common a shared understanding of the gospel of Jesus Christ, of the church's mission, and of the Christian commitment to evangelism." These conference texts are drawn on freely in what follows.

A key consensual statement expressing broadly accepted evangelical convictions throughout the English-speaking world is The Gospel of Jesus Christ: An Evangelical Celebration. Produced in 1999, it commands the widest range of evangelical leaders' signatures (from magisterial and charismatic, Reformed and Arminian, Baptist and Paedobaptist traditions) of any document included here. Earlier evangelical statements had centered on the authority of Scripture, Christian worship, political ethics, social responsibility and the environment, as well as on evangelization, but this was the first to focus primarily on the gospel itself and, more particularly, on the specifics of justification by faith.

Other faith statements drawn on in the pages that follow are those of the World Evangelical Alliance, InterVarsity Christian Fellowship, Christianity Today and World Vision. Also, we cite from the doctrinal bases of some international and transdenominational theological schools, such as Fuller, Trinity, Gordon-Conwell, Asbury and Tyndale in North America and international analogues to them, Japan Bible Seminary, China Graduate School of Theology, London Bible College and France's Faculté Libre de Théologie Evangélique. We also extract from such special statements as the Chicago Call, the Society for Pentecostal Studies, Arab World Ministries, Christian Witness to the Jewish People and the 1978 Statement of the International Council on Biblical Inerrancy, in addition to the DuPage Declaration of the Association for Church Renewal, which arose out of special need to combat softenings and dilutions of the gospel in mainline churches.

Some of our documents come from colleges and universities committed to evangelical teaching. The following positioning declaration is a typical example:

> The doctrinal statement of Wheaton College, reaffirmed annually by its Board of Trustees, faculty, and staff, provides a summary of biblical doctrine that is consonant with Evangelical Christianity. The statement accordingly reaffirms salient features of the historic Christian creeds, thereby identifying the College not only with the Scriptures but also with the Reformers and the Evangelical movement of recent years.

The World Vision Mission Statement is one that has emerged out of the context of international social services rendered by evangelicals.

> World Vision is an international partnership of Christians whose mission is to follow our Lord and Savior Jesus Christ in working with the poor and oppressed to promote human transformation, seek justice and bear witness to the good news of the Kingdom of God.

Distinguishable tendencies and motivations appear in these documents. Some simply declare what evangelicals believe. Some are framed as acts of commitment to evangelical goals and tasks. Some identify institutions as standing firmly within the arena of evangelical consensus. We use them all as resources for defining what, today, that consensus actually states about itself. Our purpose is not exhaustively to treat every issue but selectively to put in order those that best convey the evangelical consensus in its broadest and clearest terms.

1

The Good News

The Heart of the Gospel

The heart of the biblical message is the good news of God's salvation, which comes by grace alone through faith in the risen Lord Jesus Christ and His atoning death on the cross for our sins.

AMSTERDAM AFFIRMATIONS 1983

1. The Gospel

The plan of God from eternity. The gospel is the good news of God's salvation from the power of evil, the establishment of his eternal kingdom and his final victory over everything which defies his purpose. In his love God purposed to do this before the world began and effected his liberating plan over sin, death and judgment through the death of our Lord Jesus Christ. It is Christ who makes us free, and unites us in his redeemed fellowship. MANILA MANIFESTO , 1989, INTRODUCTION

The gospel of God. We affirm that the Gospel entrusted to the church is, in the first instance, God's Gospel (Mk 1:14; Rom 1:1). God is its author, and he reveals it to us in and by his Word. Its authority and truth rest on him alone. We deny that the truth or authority of the Gospel derives from any human insight or invention (Gal 1:1-11). We also deny that the truth or authority of the Gospel rests on the authority of any particular church or human institution. GOSPEL OF JESUS CHRIST, AFFIRMATIONS AND DENIALS 1

Defining the gospel. The gospel is the good news of the Creator's eternal plan to share his life and love with fallen human beings through the sending of his Son Jesus Christ, the one and only Savior of the world. As the power of God for salvation, the gospel centers on the life, death, resurrection and return of Jesus and leads to a life of holiness, growth in grace and hope-filled though costly discipleship in the fellowship of the church. The gospel includes the announcement of Jesus' triumph over the powers of darkness and of his supreme lordship over the universe. AMSTERDAM DECLARATION, 2000, DEFINITIONS 6

2. THE POWER OF GOD FOR SALVATION

The power of the gospel. We affirm that the Gospel is the saving power of God in that the Gospel effects salvation to everyone who believes, without distinction (Rom 1:16). This efficacy of the Gospel is by the power of God himself (1 Cor 1:18). We deny that the power of the Gospel rests in the eloquence of the preacher, the technique of the evangelist, or the persuasion of rational argument (1 Cor 1:21; 2:1-5). GOSPEL OF JESUS CHRIST, AFFIRMATIONS AND DENIALS 2

Telling the story of Jesus. We rejoice that the living God did not abandon us to our lostness and despair. In his love he came after us in Jesus Christ to rescue and remake us. So the good news focuses on the historic person of Jesus, who came proclaiming the kingdom of God and living a life of humble service, who died for us, becoming sin and a curse in our place, and whom God vindicated by raising him from the dead. . . . We affirm that the biblical gospel is God's enduring message to our world, and we determine to defend, proclaim and embody it. MANILA MANIFESTO, 1989, A, PART OF CLAUSE 2; TWENTY-ONE AFFIRMATIONS 3

The simplicity of the good news. The Gospel of Jesus Christ is news, good news: the best and most important news that any human being ever hears. This Gospel declares the only way to know God in peace, love, and joy is through the reconciling death of Jesus Christ the risen Lord. This Gospel is the central message of the Holy Scriptures, and is the true key to understanding them. This Gospel identifies Jesus Christ, the Messiah of Israel, as the Son of God and God the Son, the second Person of the Holy Trinity, whose incarnation, ministry, death, resurrection, and ascension fulfilled the Father's saving will. His death for sins and his resurrection from the dead were promised beforehand by the prophets and attested by eyewitnesses. In God's own time and in God's own way, Jesus Christ shall return as glorious Lord and Judge of all (1 Thess 4:13-18; Mt 25:31-32). He is now giving the Holy Spirit from the Father to all those who are truly his. The three Persons of the Trinity thus combine in the work of saving sinners. This Gospel sets forth Jesus Christ as the living Savior, Master, Life, and Hope of all who put their trust in him. It tells us that the eternal destiny of all people depends on whether they are savingly related to Jesus Christ. This Gospel is the only Gospel: there is no other; and to change its substance is to pervert and indeed destroy it. This Gospel is so simple that small children can understand it, and it is so profound that studies by the wisest theologians will never exhaust its riches. GOSPEL OF JESUS CHRIST, PREAMBLE

3. SPREAD OF THE GOOD NEWS

Treasure in earthen vessels. [God] has been calling out from the world a people for himself, and sending his people back into the world to be his servants and his witnesses, for the extension of his kingdom, the building up of Christ's body, and the glory of his name. We confess with shame that we have often denied our calling and failed in our mission, by becoming conformed to the world or by withdrawing from it. Yet we rejoice that even when borne by earthen vessels the gospel is still a precious treasure. To the task of making that treasure known in the power of the Holy Spirit we desire to dedicate ourselves anew. (Is 40:28; Mt 28:19; Eph 1:11; Acts 15:14; Jn 17:6, 18; Eph 4:12; 1 Cor 5:10; Rom 12:2; 2 Cor 4:7). LAUSANNE COVENANT, 1974, PART OF CLAUSE 1

Proclaiming the gospel. Evangelism is the proclamation of the Gospel of the crucified and risen Christ, the only Redeemer of men, according to the Scriptures, with the purpose of persuading condemned and lost sinners to put their trust in God by receiving and accepting Christ as Savior through the power of the Holy Spirit, and to serve Christ as Lord in every calling of life and in the fellowship of His

Church, looking toward the day of His coming in glory. BERLIN STATEMENT, 1966 (WORLD CONGRESS ON EVANGELISM, BERLIN, 1966)

The call to witness. All Christians are called to play their part in fulfilling Jesus' Great Commission, but some believers have a special call to, and a spiritual gift for, communicating Christ and leading others to him. These we call evangelists, as does the New Testament. AMSTERDAM DECLARATION, 2000, DEFINITIONS 12

Christian presence in the world. To evangelize is to spread the good news that Jesus Christ died for our sins and was raised from the dead according to the Scriptures, and that as the reigning Lord he now offers the forgiveness of sins and the liberating gift of the Spirit to all who repent and believe. Our Christian presence in the world is indispensable to evangelism, and so is that kind of dialogue whose purpose is to listen sensitively in order to understand. But evangelism itself is the proclamation of the historical, biblical Christ as Savior and Lord, with a view to persuading people to come to him personally and so be reconciled to God. In issuing the gospel invitation we have no liberty to conceal the cost of discipleship. Jesus still calls all who would follow him to deny themselves, take up their cross, and identify themselves with his new community. The results of evangelism include obedience to Christ, incorporation into his church and responsible service in the world. (1 Cor 15:3, 4; Acts 2:32-39; Jn 20:21; 1 Cor 1:23; 2 Cor 4:5; 5:11, 20; Lk 14:25-33; Mk 8:34; Acts 2:40, 47; Mk 10:43-45). LAUSANNE COVENANT, 1974, CLAUSE 4

2

The Bible

The Authority of Holy Scripture

We affirm that in the Scriptures of the Old and New Testaments
God has given us an authoritative disclosure
of his character and will,
his redemptive acts and their meaning,
and his mandate for mission.

MANILA MANIFESTO, 1989,
TWENTY-ONE AFFIRMATIONS 2

1. The Power of the Word

God's speech to us today. We believe that through the power of the Holy Spirit, God speaks to us in the Scriptures today to accomplish His purpose of salvation in Jesus Christ. TYNDALE UNIVERSITY COLLEGE & SEMINARY

God's witness to himself. God, who is Himself Truth and speaks truth only, has inspired Holy Scripture in order thereby to reveal Himself to lost mankind through Jesus Christ as Creator and Lord, Redeemer and Judge. Holy Scripture is God's witness to Himself. CHICAGO STATEMENT ON BIBLICAL INERRANCY, 1978, SUMMARY 1

2. To All Cultures

Its dissemination in the heart language of all peoples. The Bible is indispensable to true evangelism. The Word of God itself provides both the content and authority for all evangelism. Without it there is no message to preach to the lost. People must be brought to an understanding of at least some of the basic truths contained in the Scriptures before they can make a meaningful response to the gospel. Thus we must proclaim and disseminate the Holy Scriptures in the heart language of all those who we are called to evangelize and disciple.

We pledge ourselves to keep the Scriptures at the very heart of our evangelistic outreach and message, and to remove all known language and cultural barriers to a clear understanding of the gospel on the part of our hearers. AMSTERDAM DECLARATION, 2000, CHARTER 8

The power of the written Word in every culture. We also affirm the power of God's Word to accomplish his purpose of salvation. The message of the Bible is addressed to all men and women. God's revelation in Christ and in Scripture is unchangeable and through it the Holy Spirit still speaks today. He illumines the minds of God's people in every culture to perceive its truth freshly through their own eyes and thus discloses to the whole church ever more of the many-colored wisdom of God. (2 Tim 3:16; 2 Pet 1:21; Jn 10:35; Is 55:11; 1 Cor 1:21; Rom 1:16; Mt 5:17, 18; Jude 3; Eph 1:17, 18; 3:10, 18). LAUSANNE COVENANT, 1974, PART OF CLAUSE 2

Able to save. In every age and every place, this authoritative Bible, by the Spirit's power, is efficacious for salvation through its witness to Jesus Christ. AMSTERDAM DECLARATION, 2000, DEFINITIONS 4

Preserved through time. [We believe] the Holy Spirit preserves God's Word in the church today and by it speaks God's truth to peoples of every age. ASBURY THEOLOGICAL SEMINARY

God's Word transcends human words. We affirm that God first communicated the Gospel of redemption, and not man; we declare the saving will of God and the saving work of God only because we proclaim the saving Word of God. We are persuaded that today, as in the Reformation, God's people are again being called upon to set God's Word above man's word. We rejoice that the truth of the Bible stands unshaken by human speculation, and that it remains the eternal revelation of God's nature and will for mankind. We reject all theology and criticism that refuses to bring itself under the divine authority of Holy Scripture, and all traditionalism which weakens that authority by adding to the Word of God. BERLIN STATEMENT, 1966 (WORLD CONGRESS ON EVANGELISM, BERLIN, 1966)

To be believed, obeyed and embraced. Holy Scripture, being God's own Word, written by men prepared and superintended by His Spirit, is of infallible divine authority in all matters upon which it touches: It is to be believed, as God's instruction, in all that it affirms; obeyed, as God's command, in all that it requires; embraced, as God's pledge, in all that it promises. CHICAGO STATEMENT ON BIBLICAL INERRANCY, 1978, SUMMARY 2

3. THE CANON

Authority in Christianity. The word *canon,* signifying a rule or standard, is a pointer to authority, which means the right to rule and control. Authority in Christianity belongs to God in His revelation, which means, on the one hand, Jesus Christ, the living Word, and, on the other hand, Holy Scripture, the written Word. But the authority of Christ and that of Scripture are one. As our Prophet, Christ testified that Scripture cannot be broken. As our Priest and King, He devoted His earthly life to fulfilling the law and the prophets, even dying in obedience to the words of messianic prophecy. Thus as He saw Scripture attesting Him and His authority, so by His own submission to Scripture He attested its authority. As He bowed to His Father's instruction given in His Bible (our Old Testament), so He requires His disciples to do—not, however, in isolation but in conjunction with the apostolic witness to Himself that He undertook to inspire by His gift of the Holy Spirit. So Christians show themselves faithful servants of their Lord by bowing to the divine instruction given in the prophetic and apostolic writings that together make up our Bible. CHICAGO STATEMENT ON BIBLICAL INERRANCY, 1978, EXPOSITION: AUTHORITY: CHRIST AND THE BIBLE

The providential preservation of Scripture. The Bible is the fully and uniquely inspired Word of God written (2 Tim 3:16; 2 Pet 1:20-21). It is in its entirety the Word of God, given by men inspired by God. The divine initiative, activity, and superintendence in the process of inspiration impart inerrancy to the original documents (Mt 5:18). By God's supernatural providence the sixty-six books of the Old and New Testament canon were preserved with such integrity that for all intents and purposes our translations today are based on an adequate equivalent to the autographs of Scripture. It constitutes for us today the revealed will of God in written form (Ps 119:11; Mt 4:4), and the words of Scripture are for us the Word of God (Heb 3:7). The Bible is our sufficient and final authority for faith and practice (Is 8:20; Mt 24:35; Jn 12:48). OMS INTERNATIONAL

The sixty-six books of the canon. The sixty-six canonical books of the Bible as originally written were inspired of God, hence free from error. They constitute the only infallible guide in faith and practice. CHRISTIANITY TODAY INTERNATIONAL

The canon unrevisable. It appears that the Old Testament canon had been fixed by the time of Jesus. The New Testament canon is likewise now closed, inasmuch as no new apostolic witness to the historical Christ can now be borne. No new revelation (as distinct from Spirit-given understanding of existing revelation) will be given until Christ comes again. The canon was created in principle by divine inspiration. The Church's part was to discern the canon that God had created, not to devise one of its own. CHICAGO STATEMENT ON BIBLICAL INERRANCY, 1978, EXPOSITION: AUTHORITY: CHRIST AND THE BIBLE

The rule of faith and practice. We affirm the divine inspiration, truthfulness and authority of both Old and New Testament Scriptures in their entirety as the only written Word of God, without error in all that it affirms, and the only infallible rule of faith and practice. LAUSANNE COVENANT, 1974, PART OF CLAUSE 2

Its original form free from error. [We confess] the divine inspiration and sovereign authority of the Bible which is the Word of God exempt from error in its original form (exempte d'erreur dans les originaux). LA FACULTÉ LIBRE DE THÉOLOGIE EVANGÉLIQUE (VAUX-SUR-SEINE, FRANCE)

Preserve modesty in claims of infallibility. We stand in full fellowship with the apostles, the Reformers, and the Evangelical missioners of the centuries. None of us denies the infallibility of the Bible; none of us claims the infallibility of our faculty. We are not perfect. We do not have to be. We have God's sure Word to guide and correct our steps; we have Christ's sure grace to forgive our errors; we have the churches' continued goodwill as, to the glory of God, we fulfill our mission and theirs. FULLER THEOLOGICAL SEMINARY: WHAT WE BELIEVE AND TEACH

4. AUTHORSHIP

The ultimate Author. At Sinai God wrote the terms of His covenant on tablets of stone as His enduring witness and for lasting accessibility, and throughout the period of prophetic and apostolic revelation He prompted men to write the messages given to and through them, along with celebratory records of His dealings with His people, plus moral reflections on covenant life and forms of praise and prayer for covenant mercy. The theological reality of inspiration in the producing of Biblical documents corresponds to that of spoken prophecies: Although the human writers' personalities were expressed in what they wrote, the words were divinely constituted. Thus what Scripture says, God says; its authority is His authority, for He is its ultimate Author, having given it through the minds and words of chosen and prepared men who in freedom and faithfulness "spoke from God as they were carried along by the Holy Spirit" (1 Pet 1:21). Holy Scripture must be acknowledged as the Word of God by virtue of its divine origin. CHICAGO STATEMENT ON BIBLICAL INERRANCY, 1978, EXPOSITION: CREATION, REVELATION AND INSPIRATION

Human language as vehicle of revelation. We affirm that God who made mankind in His image has used language as a means of revelation. We deny that human language is so limited by our creatureliness that it is rendered inadequate as a vehicle for divine revelation. We further deny that the corruption of human culture and language through sin has thwarted God's work of inspiration. CHICAGO STATEMENT ON BIBLICAL INERRANCY, 1978, ARTICLE IV

Its supreme authority on all matters on which it speaks. The sole basis of our beliefs is the Bible, God's infallible written Word, the sixty-six books of the Old and New Testaments. We believe that it was uniquely, verbally and fully inspired by the Holy Spirit and that it was written without error (inerrant) in the original manuscripts. It is the supreme and final authority in all matters on which it speaks. CAMPUS CRUSADE FOR CHRIST

Divine inspiration refracted through different personalities. We affirm that inspiration was the work in which God by His Spirit, through human writers, gave us His Word. The origin of Scripture is divine. The mode of divine inspiration remains largely a mystery to us. We deny that inspiration can be reduced to human insight, or to heightened states of consciousness of any kind.

We affirm that God in His work of inspiration utilized the distinctive personalities and literary styles of the writers whom He had chosen and prepared. We deny that God, in causing these writers to use the very words that He chose, overrode their personalities.

We affirm that inspiration, though not conferring omniscience, guaranteed true and trustworthy utterance on all matters of which the Biblical authors were moved to speak and write. We deny that the finitude or fallenness of these writers, by necessity or otherwise, introduced distortion or falsehood into God's Word.

We affirm that inspiration, strictly speaking, applies only to the autographic text of Scripture, which in the providence of God can be ascertained from available manuscripts with great accuracy. We further affirm that copies and translations of Scripture are the Word of God to the extent that they faithfully represent the original. We deny that any essential element of the Christian faith is affected by the absence of the autographs. We further deny that this absence renders the assertion of Biblical inerrancy invalid or irrelevant.

We affirm that Scripture, having been given by divine inspiration, is infallible, so that, far from misleading us, it is true and reliable in all the matters it addresses. We deny that it is possible for the Bible to be at the same time infallible and errant in its assertions. Infallibility and inerrancy may be distinguished but not separated. CHICAGO STATEMENT ON BIBLICAL INERRANCY, 1978, ARTICLES VII, VIII, IX, X, XI

5. THE SPIRIT AND THE WORD

The Spirit opens our minds. The Holy Spirit, Scripture's divine Author, both authenticates it to us by His inward witness and opens our minds to understand its meaning. CHICAGO STATEMENT ON BIBLICAL INERRANCY, 1978, SUMMARY 3

The Spirit's instruction through the Word. Through [the Word] the Holy Spirit, who inspired its writing, continues to illumine (Ps 119:18, 105, 130), instruct (2 Tim 3:16-17), convict (Heb 4:12-13), regenerate (Jas 1:18; 1 Pet 1:23), and sanctify (Jn 17:17; Eph 5:26). Whatever is not revealed in or established by the Scriptures cannot be made an article of faith essential to salvation (2 Tim 3:15-17). OMS INTERNATIONAL

The call to obey the written Word. The authority of Scripture is a key issue for the Christian Church in this and every age. Those who profess faith in Jesus Christ as Lord and Savior are called to show the reality of their discipleship by humbly and faithfully obeying God's written Word. To stray from Scripture in faith or conduct is disloyalty to our Master. Recognition of the total truth and trustworthiness of Holy Scripture is essential to a full grasp and adequate confession of its authority. CHICAGO STATEMENT ON BIBLICAL INERRANCY, 1978, PREFACE

6. THE FULLNESS OF REVELATION

The written Word in its entirety. We affirm that the written Word in its entirety is revelation given by God. We deny that the Bible is merely a witness to revelation, or only becomes revelation in encounter, or depends on the responses of men for its validity. CHICAGO STATEMENT ON BIBLICAL INERRANCY, 1978, ARTICLE III

The completeness of the revelation of God's will. We believe the Scriptures, both Old and New Testaments, to be the inspired Word of God, without error in the original writings, the complete revelation of His will for the salvation of men, and the Divine and final authority for all

Christian faith and life. TRINITY EVANGELICAL DIVINITY SCHOOL

What Scripture contains. [Scripture] contains all that God pleased to reveal to men concerning salvation. JAPAN BIBLE SEMINARY

7. INSPIRATION OF SCRIPTURE

The inspired Word of God. We believe the Bible to be the inspired, the only infallible, authoritative Word of God. NATIONAL ASSOCIATION OF EVANGELICALS : STATEMENT OF FAITH

Entire trustworthiness. [We believe in] the divine inspiration of Holy Scripture and its consequent entire trustworthiness and supreme authority in all matters of faith and conduct. WORD IN ACTION (BATH CONVENTION, KESWICK CONVENTION)

The whole Bible and its parts. We affirm that the whole of Scripture and all its parts, down to the very words of the original, were given by divine inspiration. We deny that the inspiration of Scripture can rightly be affirmed of the whole without the parts, or of some parts but not the whole. CHICAGO STATEMENT ON BIBLICAL INERRANCY, 1978, ARTICLE VI

8. REVELATION IN HISTORY

The whole of history encompassed in biblical revelation. When Adam fell, the Creator did not abandon mankind to final judgment but promised salvation and began to reveal Himself as Redeemer in a sequence of historical events centering on Abraham's family and culminating in the life, death, resurrection, present heavenly ministry and promised return of Jesus Christ. Within this frame God has from time to time spoken specific words of judgment and mercy, promise and command, to sinful human beings, so drawing them into a covenant relation of mutual commitment between Him and them in which He blesses them with gifts of grace and they bless Him in responsive adoration. Moses, whom God used as mediator to carry His words to His people at the time of the exodus, stands at the head of a long line of prophets in whose mouths and writings God put His words for delivery to Israel. God's purpose in this succession of messages was to maintain His covenant by causing His people to know His name—that is, His nature—and His will both of precept and purpose in the present and for the future. This line of prophetic spokesmen from God came to completion in Jesus Christ, God's incarnate Word, who was Himself a prophet—more than a prophet, but not less—and in the apostles and prophets of the first Christian generation. CHICAGO STATEMENT ON BIBLICAL INERRANCY, 1978, EXPOSITION: CREATION, REVELATION AND INSPIRATION

The cohesion of God's revelation in history. We affirm that God's revelation in the Holy Scriptures was progressive. We deny that later revelation, which may fulfill earlier revelation, ever corrects or contradicts it. We further deny that any normative revelation has been given since the completion of the New Testament writings. CHICAGO STATEMENT ON BIBLICAL INERRANCY, 1978, ARTICLE V

9. THE SCOPE OF BIBLICAL AUTHORITY

All matters of faith and conduct. We believe in the Holy Scriptures as originally given by God, divinely inspired, infallible, entirely trustworthy; and the supreme authority in all matters of faith and conduct. WORLD EVANGELICAL ALLIANCE

Its authority for belief and behavior. It is the supreme authority in all matters of belief and behavior. UNIVERSITIES AND COLLEGES CHRISTIAN FELLOWSHIP (UCCF—UK)

The source of Christian teaching. The Holy Bible is the inspired, infallible and authoritative source of Christian doctrine and precept. REGENT UNIVERSITY (VIRGINIA)

Submitting to its authority. We believe that the Bible is God's authoritative and inspired Word. It is without error in all its teachings, including creation, history, its own origins, and salvation. Christians must submit to its divine authority, both individually and corporately, in all matters of belief and conduct, which is demonstrated by true righteous living. PRISON FELLOWSHIP MINISTRIES

The judge of all we think and do. This doctrinal commitment is built on a submission to the authority of Scripture, which must stand as teacher and judge of all that we think and do. It both inspires and corrects our doctrine and our conduct. It must always be clear that for us as Evangelicals, the Scriptures outrank all of our doctrinal statements, even statements as carefully written and as strongly believed as those in the Statement of Faith. FULLER THEOLOGICAL SEMINARY: WHAT WE BELIEVE AND TEACH

10. RELIABILITY OF THE WORD

Reliable transmission of the original text through translations. Since God has nowhere promised an inerrant transmission of Scripture, it is necessary to affirm that only the autographic text of the original documents was inspired and to maintain the need of textual criticism as a means of detecting any slips that may have crept into the text in the course of its transmission. The verdict of this science, however, is that the Hebrew and Greek text appears to be amazingly well preserved, so that we are amply justified in affirming, with the Westminster Confession, a singular providence of God in this matter and in declaring that the authority of Scripture is in no way jeopardized by the fact that the copies we possess are not entirely error-free.

Similarly, no translation is or can be perfect, and all translations are an additional step away from the *autographa*. Yet the verdict of linguistic science is that English-speaking Christians, at least, are exceedingly well served in these days with a host of excellent translations and have no cause for hesitating to conclude that the true Word of God is within their reach. Indeed, in view of the frequent repetition in Scripture of the main matters with which it deals and also of the Holy Spirit's constant witness to and through the Word, no serious translation of Holy Scripture will so destroy its meaning as to render it unable to make its reader "wise for salvation through faith in Christ Jesus" (2 Tim 3:15). CHICAGO STATEMENT ON BIBLICAL INERRANCY, 1978, EXPOSITION: TRANSMISSION AND TRANSLATION

Without error. Being wholly and verbally God-given, Scripture is without error or fault in all its teaching, no less in what it states about God's acts in creation, about the events of world history, and about its own literary origins under God, than in its witness to God's saving grace in individual lives.

The authority of Scripture is inescapably impaired if this total divine inerrancy is in any way limited or disregarded, or made relative to a view of truth contrary to the Bible's own; and such lapses bring serious loss to both the individual and the Church. CHICAGO STATEMENT ON BIBLICAL INERRANCY, 1978, SUMMARY 4, 5

The meaning of inerrancy. We affirm that Scripture in its entirety is inerrant, being free from all falsehood, fraud, or deceit. We deny that Biblical infallibility and inerrancy are limited to spiritual, religious, or redemptive themes, exclusive of assertions in the fields of history and science. We further deny that scientific hypotheses about earth history may properly be used to overturn the teaching of Scripture on creation and the flood.

We affirm the propriety of using inerrancy as a theological term with reference to the complete truthfulness of Scripture. We deny that it is proper to evaluate Scripture according to standards of truth and error that are alien to its usage or purpose. We further deny that inerrancy is negated by Biblical phenomena such as a lack of modern technical precision, irregularities of grammar or spelling, observational descriptions of nature, the reporting of falsehoods, the use of hyperbole and round numbers, the topical arrangement of material, variant selections of material in parallel accounts, or the use of free citations.

We affirm the unity and internal consistency of Scripture. We deny that alleged errors and discrepancies that have not yet been resolved vitiate the truth claims of the Bible.

We affirm that the doctrine of inerrancy is grounded in the teaching of the Bible about inspiration. We deny that Jesus' teaching about Scripture may be dismissed by appeals to accommodation or to any natural limitation of His humanity.

We affirm that the doctrine of inerrancy has been integral to the Church's faith throughout its history. We deny that inerrancy is a doctrine invented by scholastic Protestantism, or is a reactionary position postulated in response to negative higher criticism. CHICAGO STATEMENT ON BIBLICAL INERRANCY, 1978, ARTICLES XII, XIII, XIV, XV, XVI

The meaning of infallibility. Holy Scripture, as the inspired Word of God witnessing authoritatively to Jesus Christ, may properly be called *infallible* and *inerrant*. These negative terms have a special value, for they explicitly safeguard crucial positive truths.

Infallible signifies the quality of neither misleading nor being misled and so safeguards in categorical terms the truth that Holy Scripture is a sure, safe and reliable rule and guide in all matters.

Similarly, *inerrant* signifies the quality of being free from all falsehood or mistake and so safeguards the truth that Holy Scripture is entirely true and trustworthy in all its assertions.

We affirm that canonical Scripture should always be interpreted on the basis that it is infallible and inerrant. However, in determining what the God-taught writer is asserting in each passage, we must pay the most careful attention to its claims and character as a human production. In inspiration, God utilized the culture and conventions of his penman's milieu, a milieu that God controls in His sovereign providence; it is misinterpretation to imagine otherwise.

So history must be treated as history, poetry as poetry, hyperbole and metaphor as hyperbole and metaphor, generalization and approximation as what they are, and so forth. Differences between literary conventions in Bible times and in ours must also be observed: Since, for instance, nonchronological narration and imprecise citation were conventional and acceptable and violated no expectations in those days, we must not regard these things as faults when we find them in Bible writers. When total precision of a particular kind was not expected nor aimed at, it is no error not to have achieved it. Scripture is inerrant, not in the sense of being absolutely precise by modern standards, but in the sense of making good its claims and achieving that measure of focused truth at which its authors aimed.

The truthfulness of Scripture is not negated by the appearance in it of irregularities of grammar or spelling, phenomenal descriptions of nature, reports of false statements (e.g., the lies of Satan), or seeming discrepancies between one passage and another. It is not right to set the so-called "phenomena" of Scripture against the teaching of Scripture about itself. Apparent inconsistencies should not be ignored. Solution of them, where this can be convincingly achieved, will encourage our faith, and where for the present no convincing solution is at hand we shall significantly honor God by trusting His assurance that His Word is true, despite these appearances, and by maintaining our confidence that one day they will be seen to have been illusions.

Inasmuch as all Scripture is the product of a single divine mind, interpretation must stay within the bounds of the analogy of Scripture and eschew hypotheses that would correct one Biblical passage by another, whether in the name of progressive relation or of the imperfect enlightenment of the inspired writer's mind.

Although Holy Scripture is nowhere culture-bound in the sense that its teaching lacks universal validity, it is sometimes culturally conditioned by the customs and conventional views of a particular period, so that the application of its principles today calls for a different sort of action. CHICAGO STATEMENT ON BIBLICAL INERRANCY, 1978, EXPOSITION: INFALLIBILITY, INERRANCY, INTERPRETATION

The Bible alone as Word of God. The Bible alone, and the Bible in its entirety, is the Word of God written and is therefore inerrant in the autographs. EVANGELICAL THEOLOGICAL SOCIETY

Safeguarding against misconstructions of inerrancy. We recognize the importance that the word inerrancy has attained in the thinking of many of our scholarly colleagues and the institutions which they serve. We appreciate the way in which most of them use the term to underscore the fact that Scripture is indeed God's trustworthy Word in all it affirms. Where inerrancy refers to what the Holy Spirit is saying to the churches through the biblical writers, we support its use. Where the focus switches to an undue emphasis on matters like chronological details, precise sequence of events, and numerical allusions, we would consider the term misleading and inappropriate. Its dangers, when improperly defined, are

1) that it implies a precision alien to the minds of the Bible writers and their own use of the Scriptures; 2) that it diverts attention from the message of salvation and the instruction in righteousness which are the Bible's key themes; 3) that it may encourage glib and artificial harmonizations rather than serious wrestling with the implication of biblical statements which may seem to disagree; 4) that it leads those who think that there is one proven error in the Bible (however minor), to regard its whole teaching as subject to doubt; 5) that too often it has undermined our confidence in the Bible by a retreat for refuge to the original manuscripts (which we do not possess) whenever problems cannot otherwise be resolved; 6) that it prompts us to an inordinate defensiveness of Scripture which seems out of keeping with the bold confidence with which the prophets, the apostles and our Lord proclaimed it. FULLER THEOLOGICAL SEMINARY: WHAT WE BELIEVE AND TEACH

Vital to sound faith. We affirm that a confession of the full authority, infallibility and inerrancy of Scripture is vital to a sound understanding of the whole of the Christian faith. We further affirm that such confession should lead to increasing conformity to the image of Christ. We deny that such confession is necessary for salvation. However, we further deny that inerrancy can be rejected without grave consequences, both to the individual and to the Church. CHICAGO STATEMENT ON BIBLICAL INERRANCY, 1978, ARTICLE XIX

11. GUARDING THE WORD

The Spirit's guidance and the gifts of scholarship.

We believe that the Old and New Testament Scriptures
are God-breathed since their writers spoke from God
as they were moved by the Holy Spirit;
hence, they are fully trustworthy in all that they affirm;
and as the written Word of God they are our supreme authority for faith and conduct.

We acknowledge the need for the Scriptures to be rightly interpreted
under the guidance of the Holy Spirit and

using the gifts of understanding and scholarship that God has given to his people.
LONDON BIBLE COLLEGE

Responding to skeptical criticism. Since the Renaissance, and more particularly since the Enlightenment, world views have been developed that involve skepticism about basic Christian tenets. Such are the agnosticism that denies that God is knowable, the rationalism that denies that He is incomprehensible, the idealism that denies that He is transcendent, and the existentialism that denies rationality in His relationships with us. When these un- and anti-Biblical principles seep into men's theologies at presuppositional levels, as today they frequently do, faithful interpretation of Holy Scripture becomes impossible. CHICAGO STATEMENT ON BIBLICAL INERRANCY, 1978, EXPOSITION: SKEPTICISM AND CRITICISM

Resisting obstinate uniformity of expression. There is . . . an urgency about the way we go about our work. We resent unnecessary distractions; we resist unbiblical diversions. Can anyone believe that all other activities should be suspended until all Evangelicals agree on precise doctrinal statements? We certainly cannot. Hundreds of missionaries are looking to us to help them get the gospel to those who have never heard it. Scores of pastors count on us to analyze the mission of their congregations so that their growth will be encouraged. And, thousands of students look to us each year to equip them for ministry in churches, in cross-cultural overseas mission and in counseling clinics. To be truly Evangelical surely means more than debating about what Evangelicals are and who deserves the name. It means getting on with the Evangelical task. We are not a lodge carefully screening its members and briefing them with secret information. We Evangelicals are part of the church, grateful for our salvation and obedient to Christ's calling. FULLER THEOLOGICAL SEMINARY: WHAT WE BELIEVE AND TEACH

Resisting unstable subjectivism. In our affirmation of the authority of Scripture as involving its total truth, we are consciously standing with Christ and His apostles, indeed with the whole Bible and with the main stream of Church history from the first days until very recently. We are concerned at the casual, inadvertent and seemingly thoughtless way in which a belief of such far-reaching importance has been given up by so many in our day.

We are conscious too that great and grave confusion results from ceasing to maintain the total truth of the Bible whose authority one professes to acknowledge. The result of taking this step is that the Bible that God gave loses its authority, and what has authority instead is a Bible reduced in content according to the demands of one's critical reasonings and in principle reducible still further once one has started. This means that at bottom independent reason now has authority, as opposed to Scriptural teaching. If this is not seen and if for the time being basic Evangelical doctrines are still held, persons denying the full truth of Scripture may claim an Evangelical identity while methodologically they have moved away from the Evangelical principle of knowledge to an unstable subjectivism, and will find it hard not to move further.

We affirm that what Scripture says, God says. May He be glorified. Amen and Amen. CHICAGO STATEMENT ON BIBLICAL INERRANCY, 1978, EXPOSITION : INERRANCY AND AUTHORITY

12. RIGHTLY DISCERNING THE WORD OF TRUTH

Cautions on interpreting Scripture. Were we to distinguish our position from that of some of our brothers and sisters who perceive their view of Scriptures as more orthodox than ours, several points could be made: 1) we would stress the need to be aware of the historical and literary process by which God brought the Word to us; 2) we would emphasize the careful attention that must be given to the historical and cultural contexts in which the various authors lived and wrote, as well as to the purposes which each had in mind—convinced as we are that the Spirit of God used the human abilities and circumstances of the writers in such a way that the Word which results is truly divine; 3) we are convinced that this investigation of the context, purpose and literary genre is essential to a correct understanding of any portion of God's Word; 4) we would urge that the emphasis be placed where the Bible itself places it—on its message of salvation and its instruction for living, not on its details of geography or science, though we acknowledge the wonderful reliability of the Bible as a historical source book; 5) we would strive to develop our doctrine of Scripture by hearing all that the Bible says, rather than by imposing on the Bible a philosophical judgment of our own as to how God ought to have inspired the Word. FULLER THEOLOGICAL SEMINARY: WHAT WE BELIEVE AND TEACH

Reliable exegesis. We affirm that the text of Scripture is to be interpreted by grammatico-historical exegesis, taking account of its literary forms and devices, and that Scripture is to interpret Scripture. We deny the legitimacy of any treatment of the text or quest for sources lying behind it that leads to relativizing, dehistoricizing, or discounting its teaching, or rejecting its claims to authorship. CHICAGO STATEMENT ON BIBLICAL INERRANCY, 1978, ARTICLE XVIII

A spiritual understanding of the whole. We believe the historical Biblical faith; the full inspiration of the Scriptures of the Old and New Testaments; their authority, sufficiency, and inerrancy, not only as containing, but as being themselves the Word of God; and the need of the teaching of the Holy Spirit for a true and spiritual understanding of the whole. ARAB WORLD MINISTRIES

Interpreting text according to context. All the books of the Old and New Testaments, given by divine inspiration, are the written Word of God, the only infallible rule of faith and practice. They are to be interpreted according to their context and purpose and in reverent obedience to the Lord who speaks through them in living power. FULLER THEOLOGICAL SEMINARY: STATEMENT OF FAITH

13. THE SINGLE FONT OF AUTHORITY

Christ and Scripture. By authenticating each other's authority, Christ and Scripture coalesce into a single fount of authority. The Biblically-interpreted Christ and the Christ-centered, Christ-proclaiming Bible are from this standpoint one. As from the fact of inspiration we infer that what Scripture says, God says, so from the revealed relation between Jesus Christ and Scripture we may equally declare that what Scripture says, Christ says. CHICAGO STATEMENT ON BIBLICAL INERRANCY, 1978, EXPOSITION: AUTHORITY: CHRIST AND THE BIBLE

The primacy of Scripture among all other sources of religious authority. We affirm that Holy Scripture is the written Word of God, the uniquely inspired testimony to God's self-disclosure in the history of biblical Israel culminating in Jesus Christ. The Scriptures of the Old and New Testaments take precedence over experience, tradition and reason and are therefore our infallible standard for faith and practice. We deny that Holy Scripture is a merely human document that records the religious experiences of a past people, that it is only an aid in understanding our experiences in the present rather than a rule that is used by the Spirit of God to direct the people of God in every age. DUPAGE DECLARATION, 1990

The unity of revelation. We believe that God has revealed Himself and His truth in the created order, in the Scriptures, and supremely in Jesus Christ; and that the Scriptures of the Old and New Testaments are verbally inspired by God and inerrant in the original writing, so that they are fully trustworthy and of supreme and final authority in all they say. WHEATON COLLEGE

14. THE CREEDS AND CONFESSIONS AS SUMMARIES OF SCRIPTURAL TEACHING

The creeds as biblical teaching summarized. Whereas a fuller general representation of our theological position is to be found in the Apostles' Creed, the Chalcedon Creed, the Heidelberg Catechism, and the Westminster Confession of Faith, and whereas the Bible is the source, the content, and the criterion of true theology, the following summarizes the basic elements of our Christian beliefs, wherein we believe: That the Bible, containing the Old and New Testaments, is the inspired and infallible Word of God, the necessary and complete revelation of His will for the salvation of men, and it is the final authority for

Christian faith and life. CHINA GRADUATE SCHOOL OF THEOLOGY

The historic creeds and confessions. This Gospel of Jesus Christ which God sets forth in the infallible Scriptures combines Jesus' own declaration of the present reality of the kingdom of God with the apostles' account of the person, place, and work of Christ, and how sinful humans benefit from it. The Patristic Rule of Faith, the historic creeds, the Reformation confessions, and the doctrinal bases of later Evangelical bodies all witness to the substance of this biblical message. GOSPEL OF JESUS CHRIST, THE GOSPEL

Scripture and church tradition. We affirm that the Holy Scriptures are to be received as the authoritative Word of God. We deny that the Scriptures receive their authority from the Church, tradition, or any other human source.

We affirm that the Scriptures are the supreme written norm by which God binds the conscience, and that the authority of the Church is subordinate to that of Scripture. We deny that Church creeds, councils, or declarations have authority greater than or equal to the authority of the Bible. CHICAGO STATEMENT ON BIBLICAL INERRANCY, 1978, ARTICLES I, II

3

The One True God

Father, Son and Holy Spirit

We affirm our belief in the one eternal God,
Creator and Lord of the world,
Father, Son and Holy Spirit,
who governs all things according to the purpose of his will.

LAUSANNE COVENANT, 1974,
PART OF CLAUSE 1

1. One God

The unity of the triune God. We believe that there is one God, eternally existent in three persons: Father, Son and Holy Spirit. National Association of Evangelicals : Statement of Faith

The living God. The one true and living God (1 Kings 8:60; Is 43:10-11; Mk 12:29, 32; 1 Thess 1:9) is the eternal, personal Spirit. He is infinite and unchangeable in power, wisdom, holiness, and love (Is 6:3; Jas 1:17). He is the Creator, Sovereign Ruler, and Preserver of all things whether visible or invisible (1 Pet 4:19; Ps 103:19; Heb 1:3). In the divine unity of His Godhead there eternally exist three Persons of one essence, perfection, and power: the Father, the Son, and the Holy Spirit (Mt 3:16-17; 28:19; 2 Cor 13:14). OMS International

God revealed. The God of whom [we speak] is the self-revealed Creator, Upholder, Governor and Lord of the universe. This God is eternal in his self-existence and unchanging in his holy love, goodness, justice, wisdom, and faithfulness to his promises. God in his own being is a community of three coequal and coeternal persons, who are revealed to us in the Bible as the Father, the Son, and the Holy Spirit. Together they are involved in an unvarying cooperative pattern in all God's relationships to and within this world. God is Lord of history, where he blesses his own people, overcomes and judges human and angelic rebels against his rule, and will finally renew the whole created order. AMSTERDAM DECLARATION, 2000, DEFINITIONS 1

2. THE ATTRIBUTES OF GOD

God's sovereignty. God is sovereign in creation, revelation, redemption and final judgment. UNIVERSITIES AND COLLEGES CHRISTIAN FELLOWSHIP (UCCF—UK)

The infinity of God. There is one God, the Creator and Preserver of all things, infinite in being and perfection. He exists eternally in three Persons: the Father, the Son and the Holy Spirit, who are of one substance and equal in power and glory. CHRISTIANITY TODAY INTERNATIONAL

The unity of God's love, judgment and mercy. [We believe] in the one God, creator and sustainer of all things, infinite in love, perfect in judgments and unchanging in mercy. ASBURY THEOLOGICAL SEMINARY

3. THE UNITY OF THE TRIUNE GOD

The uncreated Trinity. God is a Trinity, Father, Son, and Holy Spirit, each an uncreated person, one in essence, equal in power and glory. EVANGELICAL THEOLOGICAL SOCIETY

The triune mystery. We affirm the Trinitarian name of God—Father, Son and Holy Spirit. We deny that these designations are mere metaphors drawn from the cultural experience of the past and may therefore be replaced by new symbols reflecting the cultural ethos of today. DUPAGE DECLARATION, 1990

The co-eternality of the three in one God. We believe in one God, Creator and Lord of the Universe, the co-eternal Trinity; Father, Son, and Holy Spirit. PRISON FELLOWSHIP MINISTRIES

Three persons. We believe in one sovereign God, eternally existing in three persons: the everlasting Father, His only begotten Son, Jesus Christ our Lord, and the Holy Spirit, the giver of life. WHEATON COLLEGE

The distinction of the three persons. We further believe that the one God exists externally in Three Persons—the Father, the Son, and the Holy Spirit—all three having the same nature, attributes and perfections but each executing distinct but harmonious operations in the work of creation and redemption. TYNDALE UNIVERSITY COLLEGE & SEMINARY

The equality of the persons. There is one true God, eternally existing in three persons—Father, Son, and Holy Spirit—each of whom possesses equally all the attributes of Deity and the characteristics of personality. CAMPUS CRUSADE FOR CHRIST

4. CREATOR GOD

Creation by God's Word. We believe that God created the Heavens and the earth out of nothing by His spoken word, and for His own glory. WHEATON COLLEGE

Creation of all things from nothing. God created by His word all things, visible and invisible, out of nothing, the same being subject to His absolute sovereignty. JAPAN BIBLE SEMINARY

The goodness of creation. God created the universe and pronounced it good. EVANGELICAL SEMINARY OF SOUTH AFRICA

Distinguishing the Creator from the creation. We believe . . . that the triune God is the Creator, the sustainer, and the ruler of all creation, but is prior to, and distinct from it. CHINA GRADUATE SCHOOL OF THEOLOGY

5. PROVIDENCE

God's revelation in creation and history. God, who discloses himself through his creation, has savingly spoken in the words and events of redemptive history. This history is fulfilled in Jesus Christ, the incarnate Word, who is made known to us by the Holy Spirit in sacred Scripture. FULLER THEOLOGICAL SEMINARY: STATEMENT OF FAITH

God as preserver and governor. There is but one living and true God, the Creator, Preserver and Governor of all things, who is Spirit, infinite in being and in all perfections. TYNDALE UNIVERSITY COLLEGE & SEMINARY

The purposes of Providence.

We believe that the Lord our God . . .
fulfils the sovereign purposes of his providence
—in creation, revelation, redemption, judgement,
and the coming of his kingdom—
calling out from the world a people,
united to himself and to each other in love.
LONDON BIBLE COLLEGE

4

HUMAN LIFE UNDER GOD

Creation Fallen into Sin

We believe that human beings are created in the image of God as male and female and possess dignity. All people are called to glorify God, to live in relationship with God and one another, and to be stewards of the creation. We further believe that our first parents, in disobedience to God, sinned and consequently incurred physical death and spiritual separation from God, bringing sin, guilt, depravity and misery upon all humanity.

TYNDALE UNIVERSITY COLLEGE & SEMINARY

1. MAN AND WOMAN IN GOD'S IMAGE

Bearer of God's image. The Triune God, who formed all things by His creative utterances and governs all things by His Word of decree, made mankind in His own image for a life of communion with Himself, on the model of the eternal fellowship of loving communication within the Godhead. As God's image-bearer, man was to hear God's Word addressed to him and to respond in the joy of adoring obedience. Over and above God's self-disclosure in the created order and the sequence of events within it, human beings from Adam on have received verbal messages from Him, either directly, as stated in Scripture, or indirectly in the form of part or all of Scripture itself. CHICAGO CALL, 1977

Freedom in the original human condition. Man was created in the image of God (Gen 1:27) and was innocent and pure (Rom 5:12). Godlikeness included his ability to choose between right and wrong, and he was thus morally responsible (Gen 3:3; Deut 30:19; Rom 2:15). OMS INTERNATIONAL

Man and woman the crown of creation. God, by his word and for his glory, freely created the world from nothing. He made man and woman in his own image, as the crown of creation, that they might have fellowship with him. FULLER THEOLOGICAL SEMINARY: STATEMENT OF FAITH

The intrinsic dignity of men and women. Men and women have an intrinsic dignity and worth, because they were created in God's likeness to know, love and serve him. MANILA MANIFESTO , 1989, PART OF CLAUSE A.1

2. THE FALL

The tension between human dignity and sin. We believe in . . . the value and dignity of all people: created in God's image to live in love and holiness, but alienated from God and each other because of our sin and guilt, and justly subject to God's wrath. INTERVARSITY CHRISTIAN FELLOWSHIP

The fall of human creation.

We acknowledge that though God made humanity
in his own likeness and image,
conferring on us dignity and worth
and enabling us to respond to himself,
we are now members of a fallen race,
who have sinned and come short of his glory.

LONDON BIBLE COLLEGE

Temptation and the Fall. Adam, the ancestor of mankind, was created in the image of God and enjoyed a right relationship with God. However, tempted by Satan, he rejected God's command, sinned, suffered the penalty and pollution of sin, and was subjected to the control of spiritual and physical death. For that reason, all people are born with a sinful nature and are sinners in thought, word and deed. JAPAN BIBLE SEMINARY

The choice to disobey. But man chose to sin by disobeying God, and therefore was alienated from his Creator and came under divine condemnation. Thus all human beings are born with a corrupted nature and without spiritual life, and are totally incapable of pleasing God in and of themselves. GCM (GREAT COMMISSION MINISTRIES)

Consequences of the Fall. We believe that God created man and woman sinless and holy by an immediate act. Then He subjected them to a moral test. They yielded to the temptation of Satan, and by willful disobedience to God, failed to maintain that holy condition in which they were created. By this act of disobedience, depravity and death were brought upon the entire human race. Although all have inherited a sinful nature because of the sin of Adam and Eve, yet not all are guilty of their original act of disobedience. Those who perish eternally do so only because of their own sin. A most grievous sin is the refusal to acknowledge Jesus Christ as Lord and Savior. Man as a fallen creature is self-centered, self-willed, rebellious toward God, unwilling to yield to Christ, unable to break the bondage of sin, and is, therefore, under divine judgment. We believe that as children mature, their sinful nature will be manifest. When they come to know themselves to be responsible to God, they then must repent and believe in Christ in order to be saved. During their age of innocence, the sins of children are atoned for through the sacrifice of Christ Jesus. Christ Himself assured us that children are in the kingdom of God. A MENNONITE CONFESSION OF FAITH, 1990, ARTICLE 4

3. THE LOST HUMAN CONDITION

Human lostness as a necessary premise of proclaiming the gospel. We affirm that human beings, though created in the image of God, are sinful and guilty, and lost without Christ, and that this truth is a necessary preliminary to the gospel. MANILA MANIFESTO, 1989, TWENTY-ONE AFFIRMATIONS 4

The radical lostness of humanity. We affirm that the Gospel diagnoses the universal human condition as one of sinful rebellion against God, which, if unchanged, will lead each person to eternal loss under

God's condemnation. We deny any rejection of the fallenness of human nature or any assertion of the natural goodness, or divinity, of the human race. GOSPEL OF JESUS CHRIST, AFFIRMATIONS AND DENIALS 3

The rebellious human condition. Both the law and the gospel uncover a lost human condition that goes beyond any feelings of pain, misery, frustration, bondage, powerlessness, and discontent with life. The Bible reveals that all human beings are constitutionally in a state of rebellion against the God who made them, and of whom they remain dimly aware; they are alienated from him, and cut off from all the enjoyment of knowing and serving him that is the true fulfillment of human nature. We humans were made to bear God's image in an endless life of love to God and to other people, but the self-centeredness of our fallen and sinful hearts makes that impossible. Often our dishonesty leads us to use even the observance of religion to keep God at a distance, so that we can avoid having him deal with us about our ungodly self-worship. Therefore all human beings now face final condemnation by Christ the Judge, and eternal destruction, separated from the presence of the Lord.

We pledge ourselves to be faithful and compassionate in sharing with people the truth about their present spiritual state, warning them of judgment and hell that the impenitent face, and extolling the love of God who gave his Son to save us. AMSTERDAM DECLARATION, 2000, CHARTER 5

Death passing to all. Man, although created by God in His own image and likeness, fell into sin through disobedience and "so death passed upon all men, for that all have sinned" (Rom 5:12). WORLD GOSPEL MISSION

Adam's posterity. We believe . . . that the first man, Adam, was created by God in His image, but fell from his original state by sinning against God, and hence incurred upon himself and all his posterity the guilt of sin, condemnation, and death; therefore, all mankind are in need of salvation, but are totally incapable of saving themselves. CHINA GRADUATE SCHOOL OF THEOLOGY

The fallen nature that leads to sin and death. We believe that our first parents sinned by rebelling against God's revealed will and thereby incurred both physical and spiritual death, and that as a result all human beings are born with a sinful nature that leads them to sin in thought, word, and deed. WHEATON COLLEGE

4. SIN

The sinful nature distinguished from sinful deeds. By his sinful free choice Adam rebelled against God, fell from his original innocence and purity, and received a fallen and sinful nature (Rom 5:12). Each human being today is born with this sinful nature (Ps 51:5; Gal 3:22) and by his own sinful deeds has become guilty before God (Rom 3:11-23). OMS INTERNATIONAL

The broad road to destruction. But now through sin every part of their humanness has been distorted. Human beings have become self-centered, self-serving rebels, who do not love God or their neighbor as they should. In consequence, they are alienated both from their Creator and from the rest of his creation, which is the basic cause of the pain, disorientation and loneliness which so many people suffer today. Sin also frequently erupts in anti-social behavior, in violent exploitation of others, and in a depletion of the earth's resources of which God has made men and women his stewards. Humanity is guilty, without excuse, and on the broad road which leads to destruction. MANILA MANIFESTO, 1989, PART OF CLAUSE A.1

The sentence of death. God created Adam and Eve in his own image. By disobedience, they fell from their sinless state through the temptation by Satan. This fall plunged humanity into a state of sin and spiritual death, and brought upon the entire race the sentence of eternal death. From this condition we can be saved only by the grace of God, through faith, on the basis of the work of Christ, and by the agency of the Holy Spirit. CHRISTIANITY TODAY INTERNATIONAL

The universal consequences of sin. Since the fall, the whole of humankind is sinful and guilty, so that everyone is subject to God's wrath and condemnation. UNIVERSITIES AND COLLEGES CHRISTIAN FELLOWSHIP (UCCF—UK)

Divine judgment. All men everywhere are lost and face the judgment of God, and need to come to a saving knowledge of Jesus Christ through His shed blood on the cross. BILLY GRAHAM EVANGELISTIC ASSOCIATION

Learning obedience. A believer who resists the gracious working of the Holy Spirit and fails to grow in obedience is chastened in infinite love by his Heavenly Father so he may learn obedience. BACK TO THE BIBLE

5. THE WAGES OF SIN

The inability to please God in our corrupted condition. Man was originally created in the image of God. He sinned by disobeying God; thus, he was alienated from his Creator. That historic fall brought all mankind under divine condemnation. Man's nature is corrupted, and he is thus totally unable to please God. Every man is in need of regeneration and renewal by the Holy Spirit. CAMPUS CRUSADE FOR CHRIST

Incapable of return without grace. Tempted by Satan, they rebelled against God. Being estranged from their Maker, yet responsible to him, they became subject to divine wrath, inwardly depraved, and, apart from grace, incapable of returning to God. FULLER THEOLOGICAL SEMINARY: STATEMENT OF FAITH

Unresponsiveness to God. Through the Gospel we learn that we human beings, who were made for fellowship with God, are by nature—that is, "in Adam" (1 Cor 15:22)—dead in sin, unresponsive to and separated from our Maker. We are constantly twisting his truth, breaking his law, belittling his goals and standards, and offending his holiness by our unholiness, so that we truly are "without hope and without God in the world" (Rom 1:18-32, 3:9-20; Eph 2:1-3, 12). Yet God in grace took the initiative to reconcile us to himself through the sinless life and vicarious death of his beloved Son (Eph 2:4-10; Rom 3:21-24). GOSPEL OF JESUS CHRIST, THE GOSPEL

The image marred. [We believe] that human beings were created in the image of God. This image was marred in every part through the disobedience of our first parents, and fellowship with God was broken. God, by His prevenient grace, restores moral sensibility to all humankind and enables all to respond to His love and to accept His saving grace, if they will. ASBURY THEOLOGICAL SEMINARY

Dead in trespasses. Apart from the regenerating work of God, man today is lost in sin, is dead in his trespasses and sins, and is without God and without hope (2 Cor 4:3; Eph 2:1-3, 12). OMS INTERNATIONAL

Flawed human achievements under the conditions of sin. Although God's image in human beings has been corrupted, they are still capable of loving relationships, noble deeds and beautiful art. Yet even the finest human achievement is fatally flawed and cannot possibly fit anybody to enter God's presence. Men and women are also spiritual beings, but spiritual practice and self-help techniques can at the most alleviate felt needs; they cannot address the solemn realities of sin, guilt and judgment. Neither human religion, nor human righteousness, nor sociopolitical programs can save people. Self-salvation of every kind is impossible. Left to themselves, human beings are lost forever. MANILA MANIFESTO, 1989, PART OF CLAUSE A.1

The powerlessness of man to save himself. Man was created in the image of God but, as a result of sin, is lost and powerless to save himself. REGENT UNIVERSITY (VIRGINIA)

God's love and judgment. God loves every human being, who, apart from faith in Christ, is under God's judgment and destined for hell. AMSTERDAM AFFIRMATIONS 1983

The folly of optimism. So we repudiate false gospels which deny human sin, divine judgment, the deity and incarnation of Jesus Christ, and the necessity of the cross and resurrection. We also reject half-gospels, which minimize sin and confuse God's grace with human self-effort. We confess that we ourselves have sometimes trivialized the gospel. But we determine in our evangelism to remember God's radical diagnosis and his equally radical remedy. MANILA MANIFESTO, 1989, PART OF CLAUSE A.1

6. MARRIAGE, FAMILY AND THE VALUE OF LIFE

The sanctity of human life. We affirm the sanctity of human life at every stage based on our creation in the image of God and our election by

God for service in his kingdom. We deny, for example, that the personal choice of either parent takes precedence over the right of the unborn child to life in the service of God's glory. We deplore the continuing traffic of abortion as the slaughter of innocents, which can only be an abomination in the sight of God. DUPAGE DECLARATION, 1990

Godly sexuality. We affirm the biblical guidelines for human sexuality: chastity outside of marriage, lifelong fidelity and holiness in marriage, and celibacy for the sake of the kingdom. We deny that premarital or extramarital relations, trial marriages, cohabitation outside of marriage, homosexual relations and so-called homosexual unions, can ever be in genuine accord with the will and purpose of God for his people. DUPAGE DECLARATION, 1990

Gifts to both women and men. We affirm that the gifts of the Spirit are distributed to all God's people, women and men, and that their partnership in evangelization must be welcomed for the common good. MANILA MANIFESTO, 1989, TWENTY-ONE AFFIRMATIONS 14

The relation of men and women. God created men and women as equal bearers of his image, accepts them equally in Christ and poured out his Spirit on all flesh, sons and daughters alike. In addition, because the Holy Spirit distributes his gifts to women as well as to men, they must be given opportunities to exercise their gifts. We celebrate their distinguished record in the history of missions and are convinced that God calls women to similar roles today. Even though we are not fully agreed what forms their leadership should take, we do agree about the partnership in world evangelization which God intends men and women to enjoy. MANILA MANIFESTO, 1989, PART OF CLAUSE B.6

Equality within difference. We believe [that] in the order of creation God has fitted man and woman for different functions. Man has been given a primary leadership role; woman is especially fitted for nurture and service. We believe that, in their relation to the Lord, men and women are equal, for in Christ there is neither male nor female. Being in Christ does not nullify their natural endowments, either in the home or in the church. A MENNONITE CONFESSION OF FAITH, 1990, ARTICLE 14

Marriage and the home. We believe God instituted only heterosexual marriage at the beginning of human history according to the Genesis account of creation. By this He ordained that man shall leave his father and mother and cleave to his wife, and the two shall become one flesh in love and mutual submission. It is God's will that marriage be monogamous, holy, and indissoluble, except by death. Christians should marry only in the Lord, and for the sake of spiritual unity in the home they should become members of the same congregation. Marriage was instituted for the happiness of the husband and the wife and for the procreation and Christian nurture of children. A MENNONITE CONFESSION OF FAITH, 1990, ARTICLE 15

The gift of the family. Our families are a responsibility given to us by God, and are a sacred trust to be kept as faithfully as our call to minister to others. AMSTERDAM AFFIRMATIONS 1983

Discipling children. We gratefully recognize that children and young people enrich the church's worship and outreach by their enthusiasm and faith. We need to train them in discipleship and evangelism, so that they may reach their own generation for Christ. MANILA MANIFESTO, 1989, PART OF CLAUSE B.6

5

Jesus Christ

His Person and Work—a Summary

The canonical New Testament sets forth and the historic Christian creeds and confessions attest: He was, and is, the second person of the triune Godhead, now and forever incarnate. He was virgin-born, lived a life of perfect godliness, died on the cross as the substitutionary sacrifice for our sins, was raised bodily from the dead, ascended into heaven, reigns now over the universe and will personally return for judgment and the renewal of all things. As the God-man, once crucified, now enthroned, he is the Lord and Savior who in love fulfills towards us the threefold mediational ministry of prophet, priest and king. His title, "Christ," proclaims him the anointed servant of God who fulfills all the Messianic hopes of the canonical Old Testament.

AMSTERDAM DECLARATION, 2000,
DEFINITIONS 2

1. His Person

The historical Christ. As the prophesied Messiah, Jesus Christ is the central theme of Scripture. The Old Testament looked ahead to Him; the New Testament looks back to His first coming and on to His second. Canonical Scripture is the divinely inspired and therefore normative witness to Christ. No hermeneutic, therefore, of which the historical Christ is not the focal point is acceptable. Holy Scripture must be treated as what it essentially is—the witness of the Father to the incarnate Son. CHICAGO STATEMENT ON BIBLICAL INERRANCY, 1978, EXPOSITION: AUTHORITY: CHRIST AND THE BIBLE

His incarnation. We affirm that Jesus Christ is God incarnate in human flesh, fully human and fully divine, different from all other human beings in kind, not simply in degree. We deny that Jesus Christ is essentially the flower of humanity, a spiritual master, a paradigm of what all human beings can become. DUPAGE DECLARATION, 1990

The Word made flesh. Jesus Christ, the Son of God who is the Word made flesh, our Prophet, Priest and King, is the ultimate Mediator of God's communication to man, as He is of all God's gifts of grace. The revelation He gave was more than verbal; He revealed the Father by His presence and His deeds as well. Yet His words were crucially important; for He was God, He spoke from the Father, and His words will judge all men at the last day. CHICAGO STATEMENT ON BIBLICAL INERRANCY, 1978, EXPOSITION: AUTHORITY: CHRIST AND THE BIBLE

2. HIS DEITY

Truly God, he became man. We believe in Jesus Christ, [who] without any change in His eternal deity (Jn 10:33-36) became man through conception of the Holy Spirit and virgin birth (Lk 1:31-35), that He died on the cross (Mk 15:23-26; Jn 19:16-18), a perfect and complete sacrifice, in our stead and for our sins according to the Scriptures (Heb 9:13-15; Eph 1:6-7). He arose bodily from the dead and ascended into heaven (1 Cor 15:3-4; Acts 1:6-11) where, at the right hand of the Majesty on High, He is now our High Priest and Advocate (Heb 2:16-17). NETWORK OF INTERNATIONAL CHRISTIAN SCHOOLS (NICS)

His deity. We affirm that faith in Jesus Christ as the divine Word (or Logos, Jn 1:1), the second Person of the Trinity, co-eternal and co-essential with the Father and the Holy Spirit (Heb 1:3), is foundational to faith in the Gospel. We deny that any view of Jesus Christ which reduces or rejects his full deity is Gospel faith or will avail to salvation. GOSPEL OF JESUS CHRIST, AFFIRMATIONS AND DENIALS 6

His miraculous conception. Jesus Christ is God, the living Word, who became flesh through His miraculous conception by the Holy Spirit and His virgin birth. Hence, He is perfect Deity and true humanity united in one person forever. CAMPUS CRUSADE FOR CHRIST

His divine sonship. Jesus Christ is the Son of God, sent by the Father, begotten by the Holy Spirit, and born of the Virgin Mary. CHINA GRADUATE SCHOOL OF THEOLOGY

3. THE UNITY OF HIS DIVINE AND HUMAN NATURE

Truly God, truly human. The Lord Jesus Christ, God's incarnate Son, is fully God; he was born of a virgin; his humanity is real and sinless; he died on the cross, was raised bodily from death and is now reigning over heaven and earth. UNIVERSITIES AND COLLEGES CHRISTIAN FELLOWSHIP (UCCF—UK)

The unity of divine and human natures. We believe that Jesus Christ, the eternal Son of God, in His incarnation, united to His divine nature a true human nature and so continues to be both God and man, in two distinct natures, but one person, forever. TYNDALE UNIVERSITY COLLEGE & SEMINARY

The two natures of Christ in one person. Jesus Christ is the eternally begotten Son, the second person of the Triune Godhead. He was eternally one with the Father (Jn 1:1; 10:30) and by the conception of the Holy Spirit was born of the virgin Mary (Lk 1:27, 35; Mt 1:20). Thus, two whole and perfect natures were forever united in one perfect personality in Jesus Christ. He is the eternal Word made flesh, the only begotten Son of the Father, and the Son of Man (Jn 1:14; Jn 3:16; Mt 16:13). He is the God-man, truly and fully God and truly and fully man. He was sinless in life (1 Jn 3:5). He and He alone was qualified to be our substitute, our Savior (1 Tim 2:5; Jude 25). OMS INTERNATIONAL

One person uniting two natures. The eternally pre-existent Son became incarnate without human father, by being born of the virgin Mary. Thus in the Lord Jesus Christ divine and human natures were united in one Person, both natures being whole, perfect and distinct. GORDON-CONWELL THEOLOGICAL SEMINARY

God visible in a body. Our Lord Jesus Christ is God visible in a body, born of the Virgin Mary. He lived a sinless human life. During his earthly ministry he did miracles. He died in our place to atone for our sins. He was buried, and on the third day arose from the dead. He ascended into Heaven. He is the only Mediator and Savior of the world. He will personally return in power and authority. EVANGELICAL SEMINARY OF SOUTH AFRICA

4. HIS HUMANITY

He is like us except without sin. We affirm that Jesus Christ is God incarnate (Jn 1:14). The virgin-born descendant of David (Rom 1:3), he had a true human nature, was subject to the Law of God (Gal 4:5), and was like us at all points, except without sin (Heb 2:17; 7:26-28). GOSPEL OF JESUS CHRIST, AFFIRMATIONS AND DENIALS 7

His sinless life. He led a sinless life, took on Himself all our sins, died and rose again, and is seated at the right hand of the Father as our mediator and advocate. BILLY GRAHAM EVANGELISTIC ASSOCIATION

Continuity of his person in his life, death and resurrection. We affirm that the Jesus of history and the Christ of glory are the same person, and that this Jesus Christ is absolutely unique, for he alone is God incarnate, our sin-bearer, the conqueror of death and the coming judge. MANILA MANIFESTO, 1989, TWENTY-ONE AFFIRMATIONS 5

His true humanity. We affirm that faith in the true humanity of Christ is essential to faith in the Gospel. We deny that anyone who rejects the humanity of Christ, his incarnation, or his sinlessness, or who maintains that these truths are not essential to the Gospel, will be saved (1 Jn 4:2-3). GOSPEL OF JESUS CHRIST, AFFIRMATIONS AND DENIALS 7

5. HIS OBEDIENCE

His obedience to the Law. He was conceived by the Holy Spirit, born of the Virgin Mary, perfectly obeyed the law of God. TYNDALE UNIVERSITY COLLEGE & SEMINARY

His perfect example. We believe in . . . Jesus Christ, fully human and fully divine, who lived as a perfect example, who assumed the judgment due sinners by dying in our place, and who was bodily raised from the dead and ascended as Savior and Lord. INTERVARSITY CHRISTIAN FELLOWSHIP

The completeness of his obedience. The only Mediator between God and humankind is Christ Jesus our Lord, God's eternal Son, who being conceived by the Holy Spirit and born of the Virgin Mary, fully shared and fulfilled our humanity in a life of perfect obedience. FULLER THEOLOGICAL SEMINARY: STATEMENT OF FAITH

In life and death. We affirm that Christ's saving work included both his life and his death on our behalf (Gal 3:13). We declare that faith in the perfect obedience of Christ by which he fulfilled all the demands of the Law of God in our behalf is essential to the Gospel. We deny that our salvation was achieved merely or exclusively by the death of Christ without reference to his life of perfect righteousness. GOSPEL OF JESUS CHRIST, AFFIRMATIONS AND DENIALS 9

6

CHRIST'S RECONCILING WORK ON THE CROSS

His Substitution for Our Sin

To effect salvation, he lived a sinless life
and died on the cross as the sinner's substitute,
shedding his blood for the remission of sins.

CHRISTIANITY TODAY INTERNATIONAL

1. OUR SINS ATONED FOR BY HIS DEATH

His crucifixion. We affirm that on the cross Jesus Christ took our place, bore our sins and died our death; and that for this reason alone God freely forgives those who are brought to repentance and faith. MANILA MANIFESTO, 1989, TWENTY-ONE AFFIRMATIONS 6

His victorious death. By his death in our stead, he revealed the divine love and upheld divine justice, removing our guilt and reconciling us to God. FULLER THEOLOGICAL SEMINARY: STATEMENT OF FAITH

The sacrificial death of the incarnate Son. [We believe in] redemption from the guilt, penalty, dominion and pollution of sin solely through the sacrificial death (as our representative and substitute) of the Lord Jesus Christ, the Incarnate Son of God. GRADUATES' CHRISTIAN FELLOWSHIP (SINGAPORE)

His vicarious atonement. [He] died on the cross as a vicarious and victorious atonement for sin and rose again bodily on the third day for our justification. TYNDALE UNIVERSITY COLLEGE & SEMINARY

His atoning work accomplished through his sacrificial death. The Father sent the Son to free us from the dominion of sin and Satan, and to make us God's children and friends. Jesus paid our penalty in our place on his cross, satisfying the retributive demands of divine justice by shedding his blood in sacrifice and so making possible justification for all who trust in him (Rom 3:25-26). The Bible describes this mighty substitutionary transaction as the achieving of ransom, reconciliation, redemption, propitiation, and conquest of evil powers (Mt 20:28; 2 Cor 5:18-21; Rom 3:23-25; Jn 12:31; Col 2:15). It secures for us a restored relationship with God that brings pardon and peace, acceptance and access, and adoption into God's family (Col 1:20; 2:13-14; Rom 5:1-2; Gal 4:4-7; 1 Pet 3:18). The faith in God and in Christ to which the Gospel calls us is a trustful outgoing of our hearts to lay hold of these promised and proffered benefits. GOSPEL OF JESUS CHRIST, THE GOSPEL

His satisfaction of divine justice. We affirm that the atonement of Christ by which, in his obedience, he offered a perfect sacrifice, propitiating the Father by paying for our sins and satisfying divine justice on our behalf according to God's eternal plan, is an essential element of the Gospel. We deny that any view of the Atonement that rejects the substitutionary satisfaction of divine justice, accomplished vicariously for believers, is compatible with the teaching of the Gospel. GOSPEL OF JESUS CHRIST, AFFIRMATIONS AND DENIALS 8

For our redemption. The Son, our Lord Jesus Christ, manifested in the flesh through the virgin birth, died on Calvary and rose again for the redemption of the human family, all of whom may be saved from sin through faith in Him. WORLD GOSPEL MISSION

2. HOW BELIEVERS PARTICIPATE IN HIS DEATH

Saving those who trust in him alone. He lived a sinless life and voluntarily atoned for the sins of men by dying on the cross as their substitute, thus satisfying divine justice and accomplishing salvation for all who trust in Him alone. CAMPUS CRUSADE FOR CHRIST

Putting sinners right with God.

The Father's holy love is shown supremely
in that he gave Jesus Christ, his only Son, for us
when, through our sinfulness and guilt, we were subject
to his wrath and condemnation;
and that his grace is shown supremely
by his putting sinners right with himself
when they place their trust in his Son.

LONDON BIBLE COLLEGE

The merits of the blood of Christ. The salvation of lost and sinful humanity is possible only through the merits of the shed blood of the Lord Jesus Christ, received by faith apart from works, and is characterized by regeneration by the Holy Spirit. EVANGELICAL FELLOWSHIP OF CANADA

His once-for-all efficacious atonement. Jesus Christ made a full atonement for the sins of the whole world (1 Jn 2:2) by shedding His own blood upon the cross as a perfect and sufficient sacrifice (Heb 9:13, 14, 26). His sacrifice need never be repeated nor anything added to it, for He accomplished salvation once and for all (Heb 10:10, 14, 15; Jn 19:30). His vicarious death is the only ground for our salvation (Acts 4:12; 1 Cor 3:11; 15:3). It is a sufficient atonement for the sins of the whole world (1 Tim 2:6; 4:10). This atonement is efficacious for the salvation of little children in their innocency and for those irresponsible (Rom 2:15; 5:13; Mt 19:13-15). It is efficacious for those who have reached the age of accountability only when they repent and believe the Gospel (Acts 3:19). OMS INTERNATIONAL

7

The Exalted Lord

His Resurrection, Ascension and Session

Having redeemed us from sin,
the third day he rose bodily from the grave,
victorious over death and the powers of darkness.
He ascended into heaven where at God's right hand,
he intercedes for his people and rules as Lord over all.

FULLER THEOLOGICAL SEMINARY:
STATEMENT OF FAITH

1. His Resurrection

How believers are united with their risen Lord. This Gospel further proclaims the bodily resurrection, ascension, and enthronement of Jesus as evidence of the efficacy of his once-for-all sacrifice for us, of the reality of his present personal ministry to us, and of the certainty of his future return to glorify us (1 Cor 15; Heb 1:1-4; 2:1-18; 4:14-16; 7:1—10:25). In the life of faith as the Gospel presents it, believers are united with their risen Lord, communing with him, and looking to him in repentance and hope for empowering through the Holy Spirit, so that henceforth they may not sin but serve him truly. GOSPEL OF JESUS CHRIST, THE GOSPEL

The resurrection of the crucified. We believe in the resurrection of the crucified body of our Lord, in His ascension into heaven, and in His present life there for us as Lord of all, High Priest, and Advocate. WHEATON COLLEGE

His death and resurrection. [We believe] He died for the sins of all, taking on Himself, on behalf of sinful persons, God's judgment upon sin. In His body He rose from the grave and ascended to the right hand of the Father where he intercedes for us. ASBURY THEOLOGICAL SEMINARY

His bodily resurrection. We affirm that the bodily resurrection of Christ from the dead is essential to the biblical Gospel (1 Cor 15:14). We deny the validity of any so-called gospel that denies the historical reality of the bodily resurrection of Christ. GOSPEL OF JESUS CHRIST, AFFIRMATIONS AND DENIALS 10

The same body glorified. He rose from the dead in the same body, though glorified, in which He lived and died. CAMPUS CRUSADE FOR CHRIST

His resurrection and ours. Our Lord Jesus Christ in His literal resurrection from the dead is the living guarantee of the resurrection of all human beings; the believing saved to conscious eternal joy, and the unbelieving lost to conscious eternal punishment. WORLD GOSPEL MISSION

2. HIS ASCENSION AND SESSION

His reign. He ascended to the Father's right hand where He now reigns and intercedes for His redeemed. TYNDALE UNIVERSITY COLLEGE & SEMINARY

His ascension. He arose bodily from the dead (1 Cor 15:17, 20, 23; Phil 3:21). He ascended into heaven to the right hand of the Father, the Majesty on high (Acts 1:9, 11; Heb 1:3; 8:1), where He is now enthroned. OMS INTERNATIONAL

His sitting at the right hand of the Father. He bodily ascended into heaven and sat down at the right hand of God the Father, where He, the only mediator between God and man, makes intercession for His own. GCM (GREAT COMMISSION MINISTRIES)

3. HIS INTERCESSION

His ministry of intercession. On the third day he rose from the dead in the body which had been laid in the tomb. He ascended to the right hand of the Father, where he performs the ministry of intercession. He shall come again, personally and visibly, to complete his saving work and to consummate the eternal plan of God. CHRISTIANITY TODAY INTERNATIONAL

Our high priest. He ascended to Heaven and is sitting at the right hand of God executing His ministry as High Priest on our behalf. JAPAN BIBLE SEMINARY

Our advocate. He died on the cross as a sacrifice for our sins according to the Scriptures. Further, He arose bodily from the dead, ascended into heaven, where, at the right hand of the Majesty on High, He now is our High Priest and Advocate. TRINITY EVANGELICAL DIVINITY SCHOOL

The promise of his coming again. He will return from heaven in a second personal advent prior to His millennial kingdom (Acts 1:11; Heb 9:28; Rev 20:6). He will be the judge of all men (Acts 10:42; 2 Tim 4:1). He will reign in righteousness and will consummate His redemptive mission (Rev 11:15; 22:12-13). This blessed hope of the Christian inspires us to holy living, to missionary witness, and to sacrificial service (Tit 2:13; Lk 19:13; Mt 16:27). OMS INTERNATIONAL

In sum. We believe in the deity of our Lord Jesus Christ, in His virgin birth, in His sinless life, in His miracles, in His vicarious and atoning death through His shed blood, in His bodily resurrection, in His ascension to the right hand of the Father, and in His personal return in power and glory. WORLD VISION

8

Justification by Grace Through Faith

The Acquittal

Justification is the gracious judicial act of God fully acquitting the repenting and believing sinner (Rom 3:24-26; 5:1). God grants full pardon of all guilt, release from the penalty of sins committed, and acceptance as righteous, not on the basis of the merits or efforts of the sinner, but upon the basis of the atonement by Jesus Christ and the faith of the sinner (Rom 3:28; Gal 2:16; Tit 3:7).

OMS International

1. Justification by Grace

The crediting of God's righteousness to sinners. God's justification of those who trust him, according to the Gospel, is a decisive transition, here and now, from a state of condemnation and wrath because of their sins to one of acceptance and favor by virtue of Jesus' flawless obedience culminating in his voluntary sin-bearing death. God "justifies the wicked" (ungodly: Rom 4:5) by imputing (reckoning, crediting, counting, accounting) righteousness to them and ceasing to count their sins against them (Rom 4:1-8). Sinners receive through faith in Christ alone "the gift of righteousness" (Rom 1:17; 5:17; Phil 3:9) and thus become "the righteousness of God" in him who was "made sin" for them (2 Cor 5:21). As our sins were reckoned to Christ, so Christ's righteousness is reckoned to us. This is justification by the imputation of Christ's righteousness. All we bring to the transaction is our need of it. Gospel of

JESUS CHRIST, THE GOSPEL; AFFIRMATIONS AND DENIALS 11

This teaching intrinsic to the gospel. We affirm that the biblical doctrine of justification by faith alone in Christ alone is essential to the Gospel (Rom 3:28; 4:5; Gal 2:16). We deny that any person can believe the biblical Gospel and at the same time reject the apostolic teaching of justification by faith alone in Christ alone. We also deny that there is more than one true Gospel (Gal 1:6-9). GOSPEL OF JESUS CHRIST, THE GOSPEL; AFFIRMATIONS AND DENIALS 11

The accounting of our sins to Christ and his righteousness to us. We affirm that the doctrine of the imputation (reckoning or counting) both of our sins to Christ and of his righteousness to us, whereby our sins are fully forgiven and we are fully accepted, is essential to the biblical Gospel (2 Cor 5:19-21). We deny that we are justified by the righteousness of Christ infused into us or by any righteousness that is thought to inhere within us. We affirm that the righteousness of Christ by which we are justified is properly his own, which he achieved apart from us, in and by his perfect obedience. This righteousness is counted, reckoned, or imputed to us by the forensic (that is, legal) declaration of God, as the sole ground of our justification. We deny that any works we perform at any stage of our existence add to the merit of Christ or earn for us any merit that contributes in any way to the ground of our justification (Gal 2:16; Eph 2:8-9; Tit 3:5). GOSPEL OF JESUS CHRIST, AFFIRMATIONS AND DENIALS 12, 13

The plenary pardon of all repented sins. Those who believe in Christ are pardoned all their sins and accepted in God's sight only because of the righteousness of Christ credited to them; this justification is God's act of undeserved mercy, received solely by trust in him and not by their own efforts. UNIVERSITIES AND COLLEGES CHRISTIAN FELLOWSHIP (UCCF—UK)

2. THROUGH FAITH ALONE

Grace alone through faith alone. We affirm that, while all believers are indwelt by the Holy Spirit and are in the process of being made holy and conformed to the image of Christ, those consequences of justification are not its ground. God declares us just, remits our sins, and adopts us as his children, by his grace alone, and through faith alone, because of Christ alone, while we are still sinners (Rom 4:5). We deny that believers must be inherently righteous by virtue of their cooperation with God's life-transforming grace before God will declare them justified in Christ. We are justified while we are still sinners. GOSPEL OF JESUS CHRIST, AFFIRMATIONS AND DENIALS 14

Faith in Christ alone. [We believe in] justification by God's grace to all who repent and put their faith in Jesus Christ alone for salvation. INTERVARSITY CHRISTIAN FELLOWSHIP

Faith as the fruit of grace. Our faith in the God who bestows it, the Father, the Son, and the Holy Spirit, is itself the fruit of God's grace. Faith links us savingly to Jesus, but inasmuch as it involves an acknowledgment that we have no merit of our own, it is confessedly not a meritorious work. GOSPEL OF JESUS CHRIST, THE GOSPEL

Personal trust in him. We affirm that saving faith includes mental assent to the content of the Gospel, acknowledgment of our own sin and need, and personal trust and reliance upon Christ and his work. We deny that saving faith includes only mental acceptance of the Gospel, and that justification is secured by a mere outward profession of faith. We further deny that any element of saving faith is a meritorious work or earns salvation for us. GOSPEL OF JESUS CHRIST, AFFIRMATIONS AND DENIALS 16

3. REPENTANCE

Defining repentance. Repentance is that godly sorrow for sin which results from the convicting work of the Holy Spirit (Jn 16:7-11; 2 Cor 7:9). It involves a sensing of personal guilt before God (Ps 51:4), a voluntary turning away from sin (Acts 26:20; Is 55:7), and the confessing of sin and making restitution where possible (Prov 28:13; 1 Jn 1:9; Ezek 33:15; Lk 19:8). It is the essential preparation (Mk 1:15; Mt 3:8; Acts 3:19; 20:21; 26:20) for saving faith—the simple trust in Christ for salvation (Jn 20:31; Rom 1:16; Eph 2:8; 1 Cor 12:13). . . . From that moment the believer has the Holy Spirit as his helper and witness (Jn 14:26; Rom 8:9, 15-16). OMS INTERNATIONAL

God alone able to turn sinners from sin. We need and desire to be filled and controlled by the Holy Spirit as we bear witness to the Gospel of Jesus Christ, because God alone can turn sinners from their sin and bring them to everlasting life. AMSTERDAM AFFIRMATIONS 1983

Our turning to God. The Holy Spirit alone makes the work of Christ effective to individual sinners, enabling them to turn to God from their sin and to trust in Jesus Christ. UNIVERSITIES AND COLLEGES CHRISTIAN FELLOWSHIP (UCCF—UK)

Preaching repentance. John the Baptist preached repentance, Jesus proclaimed it, and the Apostles emphasized it to both Jews and Gentiles. (Acts 2:38; 11:18; 17:30). GOSPEL CONNECTION INTERNATIONAL

4. RELEASE FROM BONDAGE TO SIN

His triumph over all evil. We believe that the Lord Jesus Christ died for our sins, according to the Scriptures, as a representative and substitutionary sacrifice, triumphing over all evil; and that all who believe in Him are justified by His shed blood and forgiven of all their sins. WHEATON COLLEGE

Release from bondage to sin. Because of the substitutionary death of our Lord Jesus Christ, God justifies all who believe in Him, forgives them their sin and its penalty, and releases them from its dominion. JAPAN BIBLE SEMINARY

Whosoever shall believe. The grace of God through Jesus Christ is freely bestowed upon all men, enabling all who will to turn from sin to righteousness and through believing on Christ receive pardon and cleansing from sin (Jn 1:4, 9; Rom 5:17-18; 1 Jn 1:9). We therefore have a Gospel for all the world so that whoever will may come (Rev 22:17), whoever is thirsty may come (Jn 7:37), and whoever will can believe and have everlasting life (Jn 3:16). OMS INTERNATIONAL

5. NEW BIRTH

The regenerating work of the Spirit. Regeneration or the new birth is the gracious work of God changing the moral nature of the repentant believer from darkness to light, from nature to grace, from death to life, from bondage of sin to liberty in Christ (Acts 26:18; Rom 6:22; Eph 2:1; Tit 3:5). The believer becomes a new creature in Christ Jesus, is born of the Spirit, and enters into a life of peace with God, obedience to the will of God, and love for all (2 Cor 5:17; Rom 5:1; 6:13, 18-19). OMS INTERNATIONAL

The necessity of rebirth. We believe that for the salvation of lost and sinful people, regeneration by the Holy Spirit is absolutely essential. We believe in the present ministry of the Holy Spirit by whose indwelling the Christian is enabled to live a godly life. NATIONAL ASSOCIATION OF EVANGELICALS : STATEMENT OF FAITH

The church's constant renewal. We believe in the necessity of the work of the Holy Spirit for the individual's new birth and growth to maturity, and for the Church's constant renewal in truth, wisdom, faith, holiness, love, power, and mission. PRISON FELLOWSHIP MINISTRIES

Justifying and regenerating grace. [We believe] God graciously justifies and regenerates all who trust in Jesus Christ. Believers become children of God and begin to live in holiness through faith in Christ and the sanctifying Spirit. ASBURY THEOLOGICAL SEMINARY

Growth in grace. We believe that God in mercy and grace redeems all who repent of their sin and trust in Jesus Christ alone for their salvation, justifying them through faith in the Savior and giving them new life by the Holy Spirit. God further wills that Christians grow in grace and in the knowledge of our Lord and Savior, Jesus Christ. TYNDALE UNIVERSITY COLLEGE & SEMINARY

6. ADOPTION INTO THE FAMILY OF GOD

Becoming children of God. We believe that all who receive the Lord Jesus Christ by faith are born again of the Holy Spirit and thereby become children of God and are enabled to offer spiritual worship acceptable to God. WHEATON COLLEGE

Access to the Father. We believe . . . that men are saved by grace through faith in Christ in response to the Gospel preached, or otherwise presented, in the power of the Holy Spirit, through whom ransomed sinners become the sons of God and heirs of eternal life. . . . Jesus Christ is the only mediator between God and man; through Him and only through Him the believer has access to the Father. CHINA GRADUATE SCHOOL OF THEOLOGY

Inheritance with Christ. Adoption is the gracious act of God by which the justified and regenerated believer is constituted a son of God with the privilege of access to the Father, membership in the family of God, and inheritance with Christ (Jn 1:12; Rom 8:15, 17). Justification, regeneration, and adoption are simultaneous in the heart of the repentant believer. OMS INTERNATIONAL

Enabled to call God Father. God graciously adopts us into his family and enables us to call him Father. As we are led by the Spirit, we grow in the knowledge of the Lord, freely keeping his commandments and endeavoring so to live in the world that all may see our good works and glorify our Father who is in heaven. FULLER THEOLOGICAL SEMINARY: STATEMENT OF FAITH

9

THE MEANING OF SALVATION

God Saves Sinners

Salvation. This word means rescue from guilt, defilement, spiritual blindness and deadness, alienation from God, and certainty of eternal punishment in hell, that is everyone's condition while under sin's dominion. This deliverance involves present justification, reconciliation to God and adoption into his family, with regeneration and the sanctifying gift of the Holy Spirit leading to works of righteousness and service here and now, and a promise of full glorification in fellowship with God in the future. This involves in the present life joy, peace, freedom and the transformation of character and relationships and the guarantee of complete healing at the future resurrection of the body. We are justified by faith alone and the salvation faith brings is by grace alone, through Christ alone, for the glory of God alone.

AMSTERDAM DECLARATION, 2000,
DEFINITIONS 7

1. PAST, PRESENT AND FUTURE SALVATION

Saved from the guilt, power and presence of sin. Salvation in its full sense is from the guilt of sin in the past, the power of sin in the present, and the presence of sin in the future. Thus, while in foretaste believers enjoy salvation now, they still await its fullness (Mk 14:61-62; Heb 9:28). Salvation is a Trinitarian reality, initiated by the Father, implemented by the Son, and applied by the Holy Spirit. It has a global dimension, for God's plan is to save believers out of every tribe and tongue (Rev 5:9) to be his church, a new humanity, the people of God, the body and bride of Christ, and the community of the Holy Spirit. All the heirs of final salvation are called here and now to serve their Lord and each other in love, to share in the fellowship of Jesus' sufferings, and to work together to make Christ known to the whole world. GOSPEL OF JESUS CHRIST, THE GOSPEL

Salvation defined. We believe that salvation consists of the remission of sins, the imputation of Christ's righteousness, and the gift of eternal life received by faith alone, apart from works. INTERDENOMINATIONAL FOREIGN MISSION ASSOCIATION

2. SAVING GRACE

Salvation wholly a work of grace. The salvation of man is wholly a work of God's free grace and is not the work, in whole or in part, of human works or goodness or religious ceremony. God imputes His righteousness to those who put their faith in Christ alone for their salvation, and thereby justifies them in His sight. CAMPUS CRUSADE FOR CHRIST

Salvation not based on our works. [We believe in] the salvation of lost and sinful man through the shed blood of the Lord Jesus Christ by faith apart from works, and regeneration by the Holy Spirit. WORLD EVANGELICAL ALLIANCE

How salvation becomes effective. Salvation becomes effective when a person, by an act of faith, acknowledges Jesus Christ as his personal Savior and Lord. The benefits of this salvation include the forgiveness of sins and a new standing before God, the impartation of new life and all the privileges that accompany a new family relationship with God. The assurance of salvation as a present possession is the privilege of every believer in Christ. BACK TO THE BIBLE

Inward and outward evidence of salvation. The inward evidence of salvation is the direct witness of the Spirit (Rom 8:16). The outward evidence to all men is a life of righteousness and true holiness (Eph 4:24; Tit 2:12). INTERNATIONAL PENTECOSTAL CHURCH OF CHRIST

3. Universal Significance of Christ's Saving Work

The way. The heart of the Gospel is that our holy, loving Creator, confronted with human hostility and rebellion, has chosen in his own freedom and faithfulness to become our holy, loving Redeemer and Restorer. The Father has sent the Son to be the Savior of the world (1 Jn 4:14): it is through his one and only Son that God's one and only plan of salvation is implemented. So Peter announced: "Salvation is found in no one else, for there is no other name under heaven given to men by which we must be saved" (Acts 4:12). And Christ himself taught: "I am the way, the truth and the life. No one comes to the Father except through me" (Jn 14:6). GOSPEL OF JESUS CHRIST, THE GOSPEL

No other name. We affirm that there is only one Savior and only one gospel, although there is a wide diversity of evangelistic approaches. We recognize that all men and women have some knowledge of God through his general revelation in nature. But we deny that this can save, for men and women suppress the truth by their unrighteousness. We also reject as derogatory to Christ and the gospel every kind of syncretism and dialogue which implies that Christ speaks equally through all religions and ideologies. Jesus Christ, being himself the only God-man, who gave himself as the only ransom for sinners, is the only mediator between God and man. There is no other name by which we must be saved. All men and women are perishing because of sin, but God loves all men and women, not wishing that any should perish but that all should repent. Yet those who reject Christ repudiate the joy of salvation and condemn themselves to eternal separation from God. To proclaim Jesus as "the Savior of the world" is not to affirm that all men and women are either automatically or ultimately saved, still less to affirm that all religions offer salvation in Christ. Rather it is to proclaim God's love for a world of sinners and to invite all men and women to respond to him as Savior and Lord in the wholehearted personal commitment of repentance and faith. Jesus Christ has been exalted above every other name; we long for the day when every knee shall bow to him and every tongue shall confess him Lord (Gal 1:6-9; Rom 1:18-32; 1 Tim 2:5-6;

Acts 4:12; Jn 3:16-19; 2 Pet 3:9; 2 Thess 1:7-9; Jn 4:42; Mt 11:28; Eph 1:20-21; Phil 2:9-11). LAUSANNE COVENANT, 1974

The only ground of salvation. We believe that the shed blood of Jesus Christ and His resurrection provide the only ground for justification and salvation for all who believe, and only such as receive Jesus Christ are born of the Holy Spirit, and thus become children of God. TRINITY EVANGELICAL DIVINITY SCHOOL

Salvation by Christ through the Holy Spirit. Salvation is available only through the redemptive work of the Lord Jesus Christ. Jesus Christ and his salvation are received by repentance and faith, apart from human effort, as the Holy Spirit brings about the new birth. EVANGELICAL SEMINARY OF SOUTH AFRICA

Redemption. Sinful human beings are redeemed from the guilt, penalty and power of sin only through the sacrificial death once and for all time of their representative and substitute, Jesus Christ, the only mediator between them and God. UNIVERSITIES AND COLLEGES CHRISTIAN FELLOWSHIP (UCCF—UK)

Countering the false peace of universalism. We therefore oppose the universalistic idea that in the crucifixion and resurrection of Jesus Christ all men of all times are already born again and already have peace with him, irrespective of their knowledge of the historical saving activity of God or belief in it. Through such a misconception the evangelizing commission loses both its full, authoritative power and its urgency. Unconverted men are thereby lulled into a fatal sense of security about their eternal destiny. FRANKFURT DECLARATION, 1970

4. THE MEDIATOR

His once-for-all mediation.

We confess Jesus Christ
as Lord and God, the eternal Son of the Father;
as truly human, born of the virgin Mary;
as Servant, sinless, full of grace and truth;
as only Mediator and Savior of the whole world,

dying on the cross in our place,
representing us to God,
redeeming us from the grip, guilt and punishment of sin;
as the Second Adam, the head of a new humanity,
living a life of perfect obedience,
overcoming death and decay,
rising from the dead with a glorious body,
being taken up to be with the Father,
one day returning personally in glory and judgment
to bring eternal life to the redeemed and eternal death to the lost,
to establish a new heaven and a new earth, the home of
righteousness,
where there will be no more evil, suffering or death;
as Victor over Satan and all his forces,
rescuing us from the dominion of darkness, and
bringing us in to his own kingdom;
as the Word who makes God known.

LONDON BIBLE COLLEGE

His mediatorial work. [We believe in] our Lord Jesus Christ, God manifest in the flesh, His virgin birth, His sinless human life, His divine miracles, His vicarious and atoning death, His bodily resurrection, His ascension, His mediatorial work, and His personal return in power and glory. WORLD EVANGELICAL ALLIANCE

The one and only mediator. We believe that Jesus Christ, God's Son, was conceived by the Holy Spirit, born of the Virgin Mary, lived a sinless life, died a substitutionary atoning death on the cross, rose bodily from the dead and ascended to heaven where, as truly God and truly man, He is the only mediator between God and man. PRISON FELLOWSHIP MINISTRIES

The promise of the Spirit. God raised Him from the dead, exalted Him both as Lord and Christ, and gave Him the promise of the Holy Spirit for His Church. CHINA GRADUATE SCHOOL OF THEOLOGY

10

The Sending of the Holy Spirit

Uniting the Faithful to Christ

We believe in the Holy Spirit
who with the Father and the Son is worthy of our worship,
who convicts the world of guilt in regard to sin, righteousness and judgment,
who makes the death of Christ effective to sinners,
enabling them to turn to God in repentance
and directing their trust towards the Lord Jesus Christ;
who through the new birth unites us with Christ,
who is present within all believers;
and makes us partake in Christ's risen life,
pointing us to Jesus,
freeing us from slavery to sin,
producing in us his fruit,
granting to us his gifts, and
empowering us for service in the world.

London Bible College

1. The Person of God the Spirit

God's active presence in the world. [We believe] the Holy Spirit is God present and active in the world. The Holy Spirit was given to the church in His fullness at Pentecost. By the Spirit, Christ lives in His church, the gospel is proclaimed and the kingdom of God is manifested in the world. Asbury Theological Seminary

The Spirit applies the work of the Son. The Holy Spirit is the third Person of the Triune God. He applies to man the work of Christ. By justification and adoption we are given a right standing before God; by regeneration, sanctification, and glorification our nature is renewed. CHRISTIANITY TODAY INTERNATIONAL

The person of the Holy Spirit. Shown by the words of Jesus to be the third divine person, whose name, "Spirit," pictures the energy of breath and wind, the Holy Spirit is the dynamic personal presence of the Trinity in the processes of the created world, in the communication of divine truth, in the attesting of Jesus Christ, in the new creation through him of believers and of the church, and in ongoing fellowship and service. AMSTERDAM DECLARATION, 2000, DEFINITIONS 3

Coequality of the Spirit with the Father and Son. The Holy Spirit is the third person of the Triune Godhead. He is of one substance with the Father and the Son, from whom He has proceeded (Jn 15:26) and is coequal with Them in eternity, grace, and power. OMS INTERNATIONAL

2. THE WORK OF GOD THE SPIRIT

The ministry of the Holy Spirit. It is His ministry to glorify Jesus Christ (Jn 16:14), and He is ever present and active in the Church of Christ (Jn 14:16-17). He convicts the world of sin (Jn 16:7-8), regenerates those who repent and believe (Jn 3:7-8), and sanctifies and empowers the believers for godly living and service (Rom 15:16; Acts 1:8). OMS INTERNATIONAL

The work of God the Spirit. The Scriptures declare that God himself is the chief evangelist. For the Spirit of God is the Spirit of truth, love, holiness and power, and evangelism is impossible without him. It is he who anoints the messenger, confirms the word, prepares the hearer, convicts the sinful, enlightens the blind, gives life to the dead, enables us to repent and believe, unites us to the Body of Christ, assures us that we are God's children, leads us into Christlike character and service, and sends us out in our turn to be Christ's witnesses. In all this the Holy Spirit's main preoccupation is to glorify Jesus Christ by showing him to us and forming him in us. MANILA MANIFESTO, 1989, PART OF CLAUSE B.5

Effective empowerment. We recognize that human energy cannot replace divine activity nor can spiritual success be measured in terms of human achievement. The effectiveness of our endeavors does not lie in human expertise but in the sovereign activity of the Holy Spirit. GREAT COMMISSION MANIFESTO, 1989

Enabling trust in God's mercy. The Holy Spirit, through the proclamation of the gospel, renews our hearts, persuading us to repent of our sins and confess Jesus as Lord. By the same Spirit we are led to trust in divine mercy, whereby we are forgiven all our sins, justified by faith alone through the merit of Christ our Savior and granted the free gift of eternal life. FULLER THEOLOGICAL SEMINARY: STATEMENT OF FAITH

Guide into all truth. We believe . . . in the Holy Spirit who convicts of sin, testifies of Christ, enables the believer to live a victorious life, and guides into all truth. LIEBENZELL MISSION OF USA

3. THE INDWELLING OF THE SPIRIT

The Spirit's indwelling. We believe that the Holy Spirit indwells and gives life to believers, enables them to understand the Scriptures, empowers them for godly living, and equips them for service and witness. WHEATON COLLEGE

Infilling the believer. We believe in the present and continuing ministry of sanctification by the Holy Spirit by whose infilling the believing Christian is cleansed and empowered for a life of holiness and service. AZUSA PACIFIC UNIVERSITY

The fullness of the Spirit's ministry. The fullness of the ministry of the Holy Spirit in relation to the knowledge of Christ and the enjoyment of new life in him dates from the Pentecostal outpouring recorded in Acts 2. As the divine inspirer and interpreter of the Bible, the Spirit empowers God's people to set forth accurate, searching, life-transforming presentations of the gospel of Jesus Christ, and makes their communication a fruitful means of grace to their hearers. AMSTERDAM DECLARATION, 2000, DEFINITIONS 3

4. Life in the Spirit

The imparting of new life. The Holy Spirit has come into the world to reveal and glorify Christ and to apply the saving work of Christ to men. He convicts and draws sinners to Christ, imparts new life to them, continually indwells them from the moment of spiritual birth and seals them until the day of redemption. His fullness, power and control are appropriated in the believer's life by faith. CAMPUS CRUSADE FOR CHRIST

Receiving power to live a holy life. The Holy Spirit convicts and regenerates sinful men making them God's children, gives them the power to live a life of holy consecration and service, and molds the redeemed into the image of Christ. JAPAN BIBLE SEMINARY

Enabling a godly life. We believe in the present ministry of the Holy Spirit by whose indwelling the Christian is enabled to live a godly life. FOCUS ON THE FAMILY

The Spirit's empowerment of character and witness. The Holy Spirit lives in all those he has regenerated. He makes them increasingly Christlike in character and behavior and gives them power for their witness in the world. UNIVERSITIES AND COLLEGES CHRISTIAN FELLOWSHIP (UCCF—UK)

Bearing fruit. Every believer is called to live so in the power of the indwelling Spirit that he will not fulfill the lust of the flesh but will bear fruit to the glory of God. CAMPUS CRUSADE FOR CHRIST

Evidences of Spirit-empowered life. The Holy Spirit is His own witness in the soul (Rom 8:16; Heb 10:14-15). He evidences His holy presence primarily by imparting His holiness to the life of the believer (Ezek 36:26-27; Gal 5:16; Eph 1:4 with Rom 5:5) and producing within the believer the abundant fruit of the Spirit (Gal 5:22-25). The evidence of the Spirit-filled and Spirit-empowered life is not the presence of any one gift or manifestation (1 Cor 12:4, 5, 11). OMS INTERNATIONAL

5. The Witness of the Spirit

The witness of the Spirit. The Holy Spirit is the witness to salvation by the inner assurance He imparts to the child of God (Rom 8:16; 1 Jn 3:24;

4:13; 5:6, 10; Rom 8:9), and by the fruit of His life within the soul: peace with God (Rom 5:1; 8:1), love for the children of God (1 Jn 3:14; 4:12), joy in Christ (Rom 15:13; Gal 5:22; 1 Thess 1:6), the guidance of the Spirit (Rom 8:14), and righteous conduct (1 Jn 2:3-5; 3:9-10). Good works are the visible fruit of a life lived in Christ; they are not the condition of salvation, but the result of salvation (Eph 2:8; Jn 15:8, 16). OMS INTERNATIONAL

Work and witness. [We believe in] the Holy Spirit, by whose indwelling the believer is enabled to live a holy life, to witness and work for the Lord Jesus Christ. WORLD EVANGELICAL ALLIANCE

The fruit of the Spirit. When we have turned to God in penitent faith in the Lord Jesus Christ, we are accountable to God for living a life separated from sin and characterized by the fruit of the Spirit. It is our responsibility to contribute by word and deed to the universal spread of the Gospel. CHRISTIANITY TODAY INTERNATIONAL

Walking in the Spirit. We believe . . . that every believer is a new creature in Christ and is called to walk in the Spirit, to die unto sin, and to live unto righteousness, and thereby manifest the fruit of the Spirit, conforming himself to the image of Christ; that good works are the fruit of the Christian life, and of themselves are not ways of justification. CHINA GRADUATE SCHOOL OF THEOLOGY

Not grieving the Spirit. We affirm that the Holy Spirit's witness to Christ is indispensable to evangelism, and that without this supernatural work neither new birth nor new life is possible. . . . We repent of all self-confident attempts either to evangelize in our own strength or to dictate to the Holy Spirit. We determine in the future not to "grieve" or "quench" the Spirit, but rather to seek to spread the good news "with power, with the Holy Spirit and with deep conviction" (Eph 4:30; 1 Thess 5:19; 1 Thess 1:5). MANILA MANIFESTO, 1989, TWENTY-ONE AFFIRMATIONS 10; PART OF CLAUSE B.5

6. ASSURANCE

The great privilege of those born of God. It is the privilege of all who are born again of the Spirit to be assured of their salvation from the very moment in which they trust Christ as their Savior. This assurance is not based upon any kind of human merit, but is produced by the witness of the Holy Spirit, who confirms in the believer the testimony of God in His written Word. CAMPUS CRUSADE FOR CHRIST

The assurance of believers. We affirm that the Holy Spirit bears witness to the Scriptures, assuring believers of the truthfulness of God's written Word. We deny that this witness of the Holy Spirit operates in isolation from or against Scripture. CHICAGO STATEMENT ON BIBLICAL INERRANCY, 1978, ARTICLE XVII

The inner witness of God's Spirit with our spirit. Believers are assured that they are children of God by the inward witness of God's Spirit with their spirits, by faith in the gracious promises of God's Word, and by the fruit of the Spirit in their lives. ASBURY THEOLOGICAL SEMINARY

Trusting grace as the beginning of new life in the Spirit. The Gospel assures us that all who have entrusted their lives to Jesus Christ are born-again children of God (Jn 1:12), indwelt, empowered, and assured of their status and hope by the Holy Spirit (Rom 7:6; 8:9-17). The moment we truly believe in Christ, the Father declares us righteous in him and begins conforming us to his likeness. Genuine faith acknowledges and depends upon Jesus as Lord and shows itself in growing obedience to the divine commands, though this contributes nothing to the ground of our justification (Jas 2:14-26; Heb 6:1-12). GOSPEL OF JESUS CHRIST, THE GOSPEL

11

THE HOLY LIFE

Sanctifying Grace

By his sanctifying grace, Christ works within us through faith, renewing our fallen nature and leading us to real maturity, that measure of development which is meant by "the fullness of Christ" (Eph 4:13). The Gospel calls us to live as obedient servants of Christ and as his emissaries in the world, doing justice, loving mercy, and helping all in need, thus seeking to bear witness to the kingdom of Christ.

GOSPEL OF JESUS CHRIST, THE GOSPEL

1. SANCTIFYING GRACE

The inherent relation between justification and sanctification. We reject any view of justification which divorces it from our sanctifying union with Christ and our increasing conformity to his image through prayer, repentance, cross-bearing, and life in the Spirit. GOSPEL OF JESUS CHRIST, AFFIRMATIONS AND DENIALS 15

Responding to grace. In responding to God's grace the believer experiences thirst for God's fullness (Jn 7:37-39), humbles himself (Is 6:3-7; Rom 7:24-25), and makes a total consecration (Rom 6:13, 16, 19). In this moment of total commitment (Rom 12:1-2) and faith (Acts 26:18), the Holy Spirit cleanses the inner nature of the believer (Acts 15:9) and clothes him with His power (Lk 24:49; Acts 1:8). Christ thus baptizes with the Holy Spirit (Jn 1:33; Acts 1:4-5), fulfilling the great "promise of the Father" which is available to every Christian (Lk 24:49; Acts 1:4; 2:39). The progressive aspect of sanctification is that process of growth in Christian maturity, Christlikeness, and practical godliness which results from walking obediently in the Light (1 Jn 1:7), from spiritual nurture and discipline (Rom 12:2; 2 Cor 3:17-18), and from repeated infillings of the Holy Spirit and His continuing ministry in the cleansed and yielded believer (Acts 4:31; Eph 3:19; 5:18; Rom 8:26). OMS INTERNATIONAL

How sanctification is realized in the believer. Sanctification is realized in the believer by recognizing his identification with Christ in His death and resurrection, and by faith reckoning daily upon the fact of that union, and by offering every faculty continually to the dominion of the Holy Spirit (Rom 6:1-11, 13; 8:1, 2, 13; Gal 2:20; Phil 2:12, 13; 1 Pet 1:5). INTERNATIONAL PENTECOSTAL CHURCH OF CHRIST

Neither withdrawal from nor conformity to the world. So Jesus intends his followers neither to withdraw from the world in order to preserve their holiness, nor to lose their holiness by conforming to the world, but simultaneously to permeate the world and to retain their kingdom distinctives. Only so can they share the Good News with credibility. EVANGELISM AND SOCIAL RESPONSIBILITY, 1982

Sanctification and sin in believers. [We believe] through sanctifying grace the Holy Spirit delivers them from all rebellion toward God, and makes possible wholehearted love for God and for others. This grace does not make believers faultless nor prevent the possibility of their falling into sin. They must live daily by faith in the forgiveness and cleansing provided for them in Jesus Christ. ASBURY THEOLOGICAL SEMINARY

Continuing repentance. We affirm that saving faith results in sanctification, the transformation of life in growing conformity to Christ through the power of the Holy Spirit. Sanctification means ongoing repentance, a life of turning from sin to serve Jesus Christ in grateful reliance on him as one's Lord and Master (Gal 5:22-25; Rom 8:4, 13-14). GOSPEL OF JESUS CHRIST, AFFIRMATIONS AND DENIALS 15

2. CHRISTIAN FREEDOM

Freedom from bondage. Every true conversion involves a power encounter, in which the superior authority of Jesus Christ is demonstrated. There is no greater miracle than this, in which the believer is set free from the bondage of Satan and sin, fear and futility, darkness and death. MANILA MANIFESTO, 1989, PART OF CLAUSE B.5

Calling to service. We believe in . . . the indwelling presence and transforming power of the Holy Spirit, who gives to all believers a new life and a new calling to obedient service. INTERVARSITY CHRISTIAN FELLOWSHIP

Enabled to love. The Spirit-filled person is enabled by the indwelling Holy Spirit to love God with his whole being (Mt 22:37-38; Rom 5:5), to love his neighbor as himself (Mt 22:37-38; Rom 5:5), and to live in true holiness of life (Lk 1:75; Eph 5:25-27; Mt 5:8; Tit 2:12). OMS INTERNATIONAL

3. HOLY LIVING

Holy living. We believe in holy Christian living, and that we must have concern for the hurts and social needs of our fellowmen. We must dedicate ourselves anew to the service of our Lord and to His authority over our lives. BILLY GRAHAM EVANGELISTIC ASSOCIATION

Exemplifying the gospel. We affirm that we who proclaim the gospel must exemplify it in a life of holiness and love; otherwise our testimony loses its credibility. MANILA MANIFESTO, 1989, TWENTY-ONE AFFIRMATIONS 15

Embodying witness through a holy life. The Holy Spirit indwells, empowers and equips each believer, who is hereby obliged and enabled to live a holy life, to witness and to serve the Lord Jesus Christ in His Kingdom concerns including worship, prayer, evangelism, discipling, compassion, justice and righteousness. EVANGELICAL SEMINARY OF SOUTH AFRICA

Conforming to Christ. We believe that God expects every believer to live a life of obedience, in which every area of his life is brought under the lordship of Jesus Christ and the fruit of the Spirit becomes increasingly evident in his life. The goal of the Christian life is to be conformed to the image of Christ. This life is characterized supremely by self-giving love for God and for others. The life and character of Christ, which grows through the Holy Spirit, is noticeably distinct from the life of the world. BACK TO THE BIBLE

The Spirit enables a holy life. We believe in the present ministry of the Holy Spirit by whose indwelling the Christian is enabled to live a holy life. PENTECOSTAL /CHARISMATIC CHURCHES OF NORTH AMERICA (FORMERLY PENTECOSTAL FELLOWSHIP OF NORTH AMERICA)

4. INTEGRITY OF FAITH AND LIFE

The integrity of the witnesses. Nothing commends the gospel more eloquently than a transformed life, and nothing brings it into disrepute so much as personal inconsistency. We are charged to behave in a manner that is worthy of the gospel of Christ, and even to "adorn" it, enhancing its beauty by holy lives. For the watching world rightly seeks evidence to substantiate the claims which Christ's disciples make for him. A strong evidence is our integrity.

Our proclamation that Christ died to bring us to God appeals to people who are spiritually thirsty, but they will not believe us if we give no evidence of knowing the living God ourselves, or if our public worship lacks reality and relevance.

Our message that Christ reconciles alienated people to each other rings true only if we are seen to love and forgive one another, to serve others in humility, and to reach out beyond our own community in compassionate, costly ministry to the needy.

Our challenge to others to deny themselves, take up their cross and follow Christ will be plausible only if we ourselves have evidently died to selfish ambition, dishonesty and covetousness, and are living a life of simplicity, contentment and generosity. MANILA MANIFESTO , 1989, PART OF CLAUSE B.7

Resisting loss of integrity. We deplore the failures in Christian consistency which we see in both Christians and churches: material greed, professional pride and rivalry, competition in Christian service, jealousy of younger leaders, missionary paternalism, the lack of mutual accountability, the loss of Christian standards of sexuality, and racial, social and sexual discrimination. All this is worldliness, allowing the prevailing culture to subvert the church instead of the church challenging and changing the culture. We are deeply ashamed of the times when, both as individuals and in our Christian communities, we have affirmed Christ in word and denied him in deed. Our inconsistency deprives our witness of credibility. We acknowledge our continuing struggles and failures. But we also determine by God's grace to develop integrity in ourselves and in the church. MANILA MANIFESTO, 1989, PART OF CLAUSE B.7

Aloof from ungodliness. We believe that we are called with a holy calling to a life of separation from the world and its follies, sinful practices, and methods; further that it is the duty of the Church to keep herself aloof from all movements which seek the reformation of society independent of the merits of the death of Christ and the experiences of the new birth. 1 Pet 2:9; Tit 2:11-14; 2:15; Mt 28:19, 20; 18:15-18; Eph 4:11-16; Heb 13:17; Acts 14:21-23; 1:15-26. GARDEN CITY CONFESSION OF FAITH 1998, ARTICLE X

Stewardship integrity. So the call to a responsible life-style must not be divorced from the call to responsible witness. For the credibility of our message is seriously diminished whenever we contradict it by our lives. It is impossible with integrity to proclaim Christ's salvation if he has evidently not saved us from greed, or his lordship if we are not good stewards of our possessions, or his love if we close our hearts against the needy. AN EVANGELICAL COMMITMENT TO SIMPLE LIFE-STYLE, 1980

5. GIFTS OF THE SPIRIT

The varied gifts of the Holy Spirit. We believe in the work of God the Holy Spirit, who enlightens the mind, works regeneration, and indwells the believer, enabling him to live a holy life and to witness and work for the Lord Jesus Christ. EVANGELICAL THEOLOGICAL FACULTY (EVANGELISCHE THEOLOGISCHE FACULTEIT, BELGIUM)

Spiritual gifts. We believe that [the Holy Spirit] was sent from the Father by the Son to convict the world, to regenerate and indwell those who trust in Christ, to baptize them into the Body of Christ, to seal them for the final day of redemption, to guide them into truth, to fill them for a life of holiness and victory and to empower them for witness and service. We believe that He gives spiritual gifts to believers for the proper functioning of the Body of Christ, which is the Church. BACK TO THE BIBLE

The distribution of gifts. The Holy Spirit sovereignly bestows and distributes His gifts within His Church (1 Cor 12:11, 18). No one gift of the Spirit is distributed to all believers (1 Cor 12:29-30). Individual members of the church receive a gift of the Spirit for the purpose of ministry and the building of the Church (Eph 4:12). Sample lists of some of the gifts are listed in Rom 12:6-8 and 1 Cor 12:8-10. The Holy Spirit places priority on grace and the fruit of the Spirit above the gifts of the Spirit (1 Cor 12:31; 14:1, 12), and among the gifts He places priority on the gifts of prophecy and teaching (1 Cor 12:28; 14:1-5). Men of God thus gifted by the Spirit (apostles, prophets, evangelists, pastors, and teachers are named) become God's gift to His Church (Eph 4:11). The Holy Spirit gives detailed restrictions for the use of only one gift—speaking in tongues (1 Cor 12—14). OMS INTERNATIONAL

6. SIGNS AND WONDERS

Signs and wonders. The New Testament shows us the supernatural power of the Spirit working miracles, signs and wonders, bestowing gifts of many kinds, and overcoming the power of Satan in human lives for the advancement of the gospel. Christians agree that the power of the Holy Spirit is vitally necessary for evangelism and that openness to his ministry should mark all believers. AMSTERDAM DECLARATION, 2000, DEFINITIONS 3

Miracles. Although the miracles of Jesus were special, being signs of his Messiahship and anticipations of his perfect kingdom when all nature will be subject to him, we have no liberty to place limits on the power of the living Creator today. We reject both the skepticism which denies miracles and the presumption which demands them, both the timidity which shrinks from the fullness of the Spirit and the triumphalism which shrinks from the weakness in which Christ's power is made perfect. MANILA MANIFESTO, 1989, PART OF CLAUSE B.5

Signs of the kingdom. [One] sign of the kingdom was the healing and the nature miracles—making the blind see, the deaf hear, the lame walk, the sick whole, raising the dead (Lk 7:22), stilling the storm, and multiplying loaves and fishes. We all agree that these were not only signs pointing to the reality of the kingdom's arrival, but also anticipations of the final kingdom from which all disease, hunger, disorder and death will be forever banished. We also agree that God is still free and powerful, and performs miracles today, especially in frontier situations where the kingdom is advancing into enemy-held territory. EVANGELISM AND SOCIAL RESPONSIBILITY, 1982

Special times of revival. At special times in the history of the church, revivals and spiritual breakthroughs have been preceded by the explicit agreement and union of God's people in seasons of repentance, prayer and fasting. Today, as we seek to carry the gospel to unreached people groups in all the world, we need a deeper dependence upon God and a greater unity in prayer.

We pledge ourselves to pray faithfully to the Lord of the harvest to send out workers for his harvest field. We also pray for all those engaged in world evangelization and encourage the call to prayer in families, local churches, special assemblies, mission agencies and trans-denominational ministries. AMSTERDAM DECLARATION, 2000, CHARTER 10

Healing the sick. The believer has the privilege of asking God to heal those who are sick (Jas 5:14-15), for the Lord is interested in our bodies (1 Cor 6:13). It may not always be God's will to heal (Gal 6:11; 2 Cor 12:7-9). OMS INTERNATIONAL

Warning against magic. We call for discernment concerning magical uses of Christian terms and caution practitioners to avoid making spiritual conflict into Christian magic. Any suggestion that a particular technique or method in spiritual conflict ministry ensures success is a magical, sub-Christian understanding of God's workings. . . . We warn against using eschatology as an excuse not to fight against all forms of evil in the present. DELIVER US FROM EVIL CONSULTATION STATEMENT, 2000, WARNINGS 3, 11

7. PERSEVERING THROUGH SPIRITUAL WARFARE

Expect opposition. The records of evangelism from the apostolic age, the state of the world around us today, and the knowledge of Satan's opposition at all times to the spread of the gospel, combine to assure us that evangelistic outreach in the twenty-first century will be an advance in the midst of opposition. Current forms of opposition, which Satan evidently exploits, include secular ideologies that see Christian faith as a hindrance to human development; political power structures that see the primacy of Christians' loyalty to their Lord as a threat to the regime; and militant expressions of non-Christian religions that are hostile to Christians for being different. We must expect, and be prepared for, many kinds of suffering as we struggle not against enemies of blood and flesh, but against the spiritual forces of evil in the heavenly places.

We pledge ourselves ever to seek to move forward wisely in personal evangelism, family evangelism, local church evangelism, and cooperative evangelism in its various forms, and to persevere in this despite the opposition we may encounter. We will stand in solidarity with our brothers and sisters in Christ who suffer persecution and even martyrdom for their faithful gospel witness. AMSTERDAM DECLARATION, 2000, CHARTER 13

Spiritual warfare. We believe that we are engaged in constant spiritual warfare with the principalities and powers of evil, who are seeking to overthrow the church and frustrate its task of world evangelization. We know our need to equip ourselves with God's armor and to fight this battle with the spiritual weapons of truth and prayer. For we detect the activity of our enemy, not only in false ideologies outside the church, but also inside it in false gospels which twist Scripture and put man in the place of God. We need both watchfulness and discernment to safeguard the biblical gospel. We acknowledge that we ourselves are not immune to worldliness of thought and action, that is, to a surrender to secularism. For example, although careful studies of church growth, both numerical and spiritual, are right and valuable, we have sometimes neglected them. At other times, desirous to ensure a response to the gospel, we have compromised our message, manipulated our hearers through pressure techniques, and become unduly preoccupied with statistics or even dishonest in our use of them. All this is worldly. The church must be in the world; the world must not be in the church. (Eph 6:12; 2 Cor 4:3, 4; Eph 6:11, 13-18; 2 Cor 10:3-5; 1 Jn 2:18-26; 4:1-3; Gal 1:6-9; 2 Cor 2:17; 4:2; Jn 17:15). LAUSANNE COVENANT, 1974

The principalities and powers. We affirm that spiritual warfare demands spiritual weapons, and that we must both preach the word in the power of the Spirit, and pray constantly that we may enter into Christ's victory over the principalities and powers of evil. . . . All evangelism involves spiritual warfare with the principalities and powers of evil, in which only spiritual weapons can prevail, especially the Word and the Spirit, with prayer. We therefore call on all Christian people to be diligent in their prayers both for the renewal of the church and for the evangelization of the world. MANILA MANIFESTO, 1989, TWENTY-ONE AFFIRMATIONS 11; PART OF CLAUSE B.5

The adversary has worked throughout history. There are striking similarities between what happened from the history of the ancient church to what is happening in demonic encounters and deliverance today. Deliverance from Satanic and demonic powers and influence in the ancient church was used as proof of the resurrection and the truth of the claims of Christ by the church fathers. Preparation for baptism included the renunciation of the Devil, the demonic and prior religious allegiances from the life of the convert as well as repentance. This practice continues in some churches to this day. The unwillingness/inability of the contemporary western church to believe in the reality of the spiritual beliefs and engage in spiritual conflict arose out of a defective Enlightenment-influenced world view, and is not representative of the total history of the church in relation to spiritual conflict nor has it been characteristic of Christianity in the Two Thirds World in contemporary history. DELIVER US FROM EVIL CONSULTATION STATEMENT, 2000, SPIRITUAL CONFLICT IN PRACTICE

Kept by the power of God. Believers are kept by the power of God unto eternal salvation and are called to a life of discipleship and holiness in joyful obedience to Jesus Christ. TYNDALE UNIVERSITY COLLEGE & SEMINARY

8. OVERCOMING THE ENEMY

The defeat of Satan. We believe in the existence of Satan, sin, and evil powers, and that all these have been defeated by God in the cross of Christ. WHEATON COLLEGE

Satan's purpose. We believe in . . . the personal existence of Satan, whose intent is to supplant God and frustrate His purposes, and whose ultimate end is consignment to eternal punishment. EVANGELICAL ASSOCIATION OF THE CARIBBEAN

The great enemy. We believe in the personality and depraved character of Satan, who is the great enemy of God and man. We believe that he, along with the company of demonic beings serving him, works out his evil plans through the ungodly world system, limited only by the sovereign rule of God. We believe that he was judged by Christ at the cross and will ultimately meet his doom in the lake of fire, where he will remain eternally. BACK TO THE BIBLE

Powerful but already doomed. We believe in the reality of Satan, a created being, the enemy of God and mankind. Although powerful in this age, he is doomed by the sacrificial death of Christ. SOUTH AMERICA MISSION

The adversary fallen from original creation. We believe that Satan was originally created a perfect being. He rebelled against God. As a result he became depraved, the devil and adversary of God and His people, the leader of a host of angels who fell with him. Satan has been judged and defeated at the cross. INTERNATIONAL PENTECOSTAL CHURCH OF CHRIST

The works of the adversary. Satan and "the rulers, authorities, the powers of this dark world, the spiritual forces of evil in the heavenly realms" are at work through: Deceiving and distorting; tempting to sin; afflicting the body, emotions, mind, and will; taking control of a person; disordering of nature; distorting the roles of social, economic, and political structures; scapegoating as a means of legitimizing violence; promoting self-interest, injustice, oppression, and abuse; the realm of the occult; false religions; all forms of opposition to God's work of salvation and the mission of the church. DELIVER US FROM EVIL CONSULTATION STATEMENT, 2000, THEOLOGICAL AFFIRMATIONS 6

Abiding in Christ's fellowship. The believer is securely kept by the power of God as he abides in vital fellowship with Christ. OMS INTERNATIONAL

9. PRAYER AND SPIRITUAL DISCIPLINE

Nurturing the disciplines of the Spirit. We acknowledge our obligation, as servants of God, to lead lives of holiness and moral purity, knowing that we exemplify Christ to the church and to the world. A life of regular and faithful prayer and Bible study is essential to our personal spiritual growth, and to our power for ministry. AMSTERDAM AFFIRMATIONS 1983

The purposes of discipline. The purposes of discipline are to clarify for all members the meaning of Christian discipleship, to lead each member to full stature in Christ, to promote the purity of the church, to warn the weak and immature of the serious character of sin and disobedience to God's Word, to restore to full fellowship the members who may fall into sin, and to maintain the good name and witness of the church before the world. A MENNONITE CONFESSION OF FAITH, 1990, ARTICLE 8

Prayer. God has given us the gift of prayer so that in his sovereignty he may respond in blessing and power to the cries of his children. Prayer is an essential means God has appointed for the awakening of the church and the carrying of the gospel throughout the world. From the first days of the New Testament church, God has used the fervent, persistent praying of his people to empower their witness in the Spirit, overcome opposition to the Lord's work and open the minds and hearts of those who hear the message of Christ. AMSTERDAM DECLARATION , 2000, CHARTER 10

The call to prayer. We call on Evangelicals everywhere to pray—for unity and for the spread of the gospel . . . —worshiping and praising God, calling on him, confessing our sin and need for his grace, seeking his wisdom and counsel, interceding for others, and offering ourselves to him and his service. NATIONAL ASSOCIATION OF EVANGELICALS : AN EVANGELICAL MANIFESTO

A balanced spirituality. We suffer from a neglect of authentic spirituality on the one hand, and an excess of undisciplined spirituality on the other hand. We have too often pursued a superhuman religiosity rather than the biblical model of a true humanity released from bondage to sin and renewed by the Holy Spirit. Therefore we call for a spirituality which grasps by faith the full content of Christ's redemptive work: freedom from the guilt and power of sin, and newness of life through the indwelling and outpouring of his Spirit. We affirm the centrality of the preaching of the Word of God as a primary means by which his Spirit works to renew the church in its corporate life as well as in the individual lives of believers. A true spirituaity will call for identification with the suffering of the world as well as the cultivation of personal piety. CHICAGO CALL, 1977

12

Unity in the Truth of the Gospel

The Unity of All Believers

We believe in . . . the unity of all believers in Jesus Christ,
manifest in worshiping and witnessing churches
making disciples throughout the world.

INTERVARSITY CHRISTIAN FELLOWSHIP

1. Truth and Unity

Christian truth as the basis of Christian unity. All Christians are called to unity in love and unity in truth. As Evangelicals who derive our very name from the Gospel, we celebrate this great good news of God's saving work in Jesus Christ as the true bond of Christian unity, whether among organized churches and denominations or in the many transdenominational cooperative enterprises of Christians together. The Bible declares that all who truly trust in Christ and his Gospel are sons and daughters of God through grace, and hence are our brothers and sisters in Christ. All who are justified experience reconciliation with the Father, full remission of sins, transition from the kingdom of darkness to the kingdom of light, the reality of being a new creature in Christ, and the fellowship of the Holy Spirit. They enjoy access to the Father with all the peace and joy that this brings. The Gospel requires of all believers worship, which means constant praise and giving of thanks to God, submission to all that he has revealed in his written Word, prayerful dependence on him, and vigilance lest his truth be even inadvertently compromised or obscured. To share the joy and hope of this Gospel is a supreme privilege. It is also an abiding obligation, for the Great Commission of Jesus Christ still stands: proclaim the Gospel everywhere, he said, teaching, baptizing, and making disciples. GOSPEL OF JESUS CHRIST, PREAMBLE

Unity in truth and the façade of unity. We affirm that the church's visible unity in truth is God's purpose. Evangelism also summons us to unity, because our oneness strengthens our witness, just as our disunity undermines our gospel of reconciliation. We recognize, however, that organizational unity may take many forms and does not necessarily forward evangelism. Yet we who share the same biblical faith should be closely united in fellowship, work and witness. We confess that our testimony has sometimes been marred by sinful individualism and needless duplication. We pledge ourselves to seek a deeper unity in truth, worship, holiness and mission. We urge the development of regional and functional cooperation for the furtherance of the church's mission, for strategic planning, for mutual encouragement, and for the sharing of resources, and experience. (Jn 17:21, 23; Eph 4:3, 4; Jn 13:35; Phil 1:27; Jn 17:11-23). LAUSANNE COVENANT, 1974

Praying for the unity of the body. We beseech the Body of Christ to join with us in prayer and work for peace in our world, for revival and a renewed dedication to the biblical priority of evangelism in the church, and for the oneness of believers in Christ for the fulfillment of the Great Commission, until Christ returns. AMSTERDAM AFFIRMATIONS 1983

2. CHRISTIAN UNITY IN THE GOSPEL

The gospel and Christian unity. Evangelism and unity are closely related in the New Testament. Jesus prayed that his people's oneness might reflect his own oneness with the Father, in order that the world might believe in him, and Paul exhorted the Philippians to "contend as one person for the faith of the gospel." In contrast to this biblical vision, we are ashamed of the suspicions and rivalries, the dogmatism over non-essentials, the power-struggles and empire-building which spoil our evangelistic witness. We affirm that cooperation in evangelism is indispensable, first because it is the will of God, but also because the gospel of reconciliation is discredited by our disunity, and because, if the task of world evangelization is ever to be accomplished, we must engage in it together. MANILA MANIFESTO, 1989, PART OF CLAUSE B.9

Resolving differences between Christians. Jesus prayed to the Heavenly Father that his disciples would be one so that the world might believe. One of the great hindrances to evangelism worldwide is the lack of unity among Christ's people, a condition made worse when Christians compete and fight with one another rather than seeking together the mind of Christ. We cannot resolve all differences among Christians because we do not yet understand perfectly all that God has revealed to us. But in all ways that do not violate our conscience, we should pursue cooperation and partnerships with other believers in the task of evangelism practicing the well-tested rule of Christian fellowship: "In necessary things, unity; in non-essential things, liberty; in all things, charity."

We pledge ourselves to pray and work for unity in truth among all true believers in Jesus and to cooperate as fully as possible in evangelism with other brothers and sisters in Christ so that the whole church may take the whole gospel to the whole world. AMSTERDAM DECLARATION, 2000, CHARTER 14

Until we come in the unity of the faith. [We seek] to promote courtesy and mutual understanding, "endeavoring to keep the unity of the Spirit in the bond of peace, . . . until we all come in the unity of the faith" (Eph 4:3, 13). SOCIETY FOR PENTECOSTAL STUDIES

Freedom of conviction on nonessentials. We accept those areas of doctrinal teaching on which, historically, there has been general agreement among all true Christians. Because of the specialized calling of our movement, we desire to allow for freedom of conviction on other doctrinal matters, provided that any interpretation is based upon the Bible alone, and that no such interpretation shall become an issue which hinders the ministry to which God has called us. CAMPUS CRUSADE FOR CHRIST

Avoiding competitiveness. We affirm the urgent need for churches, mission agencies and other Christian organizations to cooperate in evangelism and social action, repudiating competition and avoiding duplication. MANILA MANIFESTO, 1989, TWENTY-ONE AFFIRMATIONS 17

Encouraging missional cooperation. We rejoice that a new missionary era has dawned. The dominant role of western missions is fast disappearing. God is raising up from the younger churches a great new resource for world evangelization, and is thus demonstrating that the responsibility to evangelize belongs to the whole body of Christ. All churches should therefore be asking God and themselves what they should be doing both to reach their own area and to send missionaries to other parts of the world. A re-evaluation of our missionary responsibility and role should be continuous. Thus a growing partnership of churches will develop and the universal character of Christ's church will be more clearly exhibited. We also thank God for agencies which labor in Bible translation, theological education, the mass media, Christian literature, evangelism, missions, church renewal and other specialist fields. (Rom 1:8; Phil 1:5; 4:15; Acts 13:1-3; 1 Thess 1:6-8). LAUSANNE COVENANT, 1974, PART OF CLAUSE 8

Promoting unity. We affirm and promote unity in the Body of Christ. We pursue relationships with all churches and desire mutual participation in ministry. We seek to contribute to the holistic mission of the church. We maintain a cooperative stance and a spirit of openness towards other humanitarian organizations. WORLD VISION

Love one another. We believe in the spiritual unity of believers in our Lord Jesus Christ. . . . "A new command I give you: Love one another. As I have loved you, so you must love one another. By this all men will know that you are my disciples, if you love one another" (Jn 13:34-35). We call on the Evangelical community to work together diligently based on our common commitment to Jesus Christ as Lord and only Savior. Furthermore, as long as the truth is not compromised, we urge Evangelicals, in a demonstration of love, to work alongside others who may not necessarily have an Evangelical identity on various specific issues. NATIONAL ASSOCIATION OF EVANGELICALS STATEMENT OF FAITH: AN EVANGELICAL MANIFESTO

The scandal of isolation. We deplore the scandalous isolation and separation of Christians from one another. We believe such division is contrary to Christ's explicit desire for unity among his people and impedes the witness of the church in the world. Evangelicalism is too frequently characterized by an ahistorical, sectarian mentality. We fail to appropriate the catholicity of historic Christianity, as well as the breadth of the biblical revelation. CHICAGO CALL, 1977

Confessing the brokenness of Christ's body. We confess our own share of responsibility for the brokenness of the Body of Christ, which is a major stumbling-block to world evangelization. We determine to go on seeking that unity in truth for which Christ prayed. MANILA MANIFESTO, 1989, PART OF CLAUSE B.9

3. MANIFESTING OUR UNITY IN CHRIST

Cooperation without compromise. We call on Evangelical denominations and movements to operate in cooperation without compromise—maintaining our particular distinctives, yet standing together on the basis of the command of our Lord Jesus Christ found in John 13:34-35. NATIONAL ASSOCIATION OF EVANGELICALS: AN EVANGELICAL MANIFESTO

Seeking visible expressions of unity in Christ. Therefore we call Evangelicals to return to the ecumenical concern of the Reformers and the later movements of Evangelical renewal. We must humbly and critically scrutinize our respective traditions, renounce sacred shibboleths, and recognize that God works within diverse historical streams. We must resist efforts promoting church union-at-any-cost, but we must also avoid mere spiritualized concepts of church unity. We are convinced that unity in Christ requires visible and concrete expressions. In this belief, we welcome the development of encounter and cooperation within Christ's church. While we seek to avoid doctrinal indifferentism and a false irenicism, we encourage Evangelicals to cultivate increased discussion and cooperation, both within and without their respective traditions, earnestly seeking common areas of agreement and understanding. CHICAGO CALL, 1977

Avoiding presumption. Our reference to "the whole church" is not a presumptuous claim that the universal church and the Evangelical community are synonymous. For we recognize that there are many churches which are not part of the Evangelical movement. . . . Where appropriate, and so long as biblical truth is not compromised, cooperation may be possible in such areas as Bible translation, the study of contemporary theological and ethical issues, social work and political action. MANILA MANIFESTO, 1989, PART OF CLAUSE B.9

Forgoing undue attachment to controversial terms. At times, some Christians have become unduly attached to the precise wordings of doctrine—whether of events in the last days, the meaning of baptism, or the use of a catch phrase like "the inerrancy of Scripture." But it is well to remember that all our formulations of Christian truth must ultimately conform not to some preset statement but to the Scriptures, all parts of which are divinely inspired. . . . As for a doctrine of Scripture, which is always pivotal to Evangelical faith, we have only one aim: to believe and to teach precisely what the Bible teaches about itself. FULLER THEOLOGICAL SEMINARY: WHAT WE BELIEVE AND TEACH

Unity and godliness. In this day, however, this critical need for greater unity and godliness among Christians is being met with a surging desire for just such a transformation. And, it is springing up across the breadth of the church. It could well be that the body of Christ is ready now to allow the pastoral prayer of the Son of God in John 17:20-23 to renew itself dramatically in our lives. "My prayer is not for them alone. I pray also for those who will believe in me through their message, that all of them may be one, Father, just as you are in me and I am in you. May they also be in us so that the world may believe that you have sent me. I have given them the glory that you gave me, that they may be one as we are one: I in them and you in me. May they be brought to complete unity to let the world know that you sent me and have loved them even as you have loved me." NATIONAL ASSOCIATION OF EVANGELICALS: AN EVANGELICAL MANIFESTO

13

THE CHURCH

The People of God

We believe that the Church is the people of God, the body of Christ and a fellowship in the Spirit of all those saved by the grace of God. We further believe that this one, holy, catholic and apostolic church expresses itself in a local body of believers and encompasses and transcends the various local, denominational and transdenominational expressions of the life of the believing community. The Church is called and sent into the world by the Triune God to declare and demonstrate the Good News of Jesus Christ in the power of the Holy Spirit.

TYNDALE UNIVERSITY COLLEGE & SEMINARY

1. MARKS OF THE CHURCH

The church as sign of the kingdom. The church is intended by God to be a sign of his kingdom, that is, an indication of what human community looks like when it comes under his rule of righteousness and peace. As with individuals, so with churches, the gospel has to be embodied if it is to be communicated effectively. It is through our love for one another that the invisible God reveals himself today, especially when our fellowship is expressed in small groups, and when it transcends the barriers of race, rank, sex and age which divide other communities.

We deeply regret that many of our congregations are inward-looking, organized for maintenance rather than mission, or preoccupied with church-based activities at the expense of witness. We determine to turn our churches inside out, so that they may engage in continuous outreach, until the Lord adds to them daily those who are being saved. MANILA MANIFESTO, 1989, PART OF CLAUSE B.8

Firstfruits of the new humanity. The church is the community in which God's kingly rule is revealed, which therefore witnesses to the divine rule, and is the firstfruits of the redeemed humanity (Jas 1:18). It lives by new values and standards, and its relationships have been transformed by love. Yet it continues to fail. For it lives in an uneasy tension between the "already" and the "not yet," between the present reality and the future expectation of the kingdom. EVANGELISM AND SOCIAL RESPONSIBILITY, 1982

God's call to covenant community. Salvation continues with the *new community.* For salvation in the Bible is never a purely individualistic concept. As in the Old Testament, so in the New, God is calling out a people for himself and binding it to himself by a solemn covenant. The members of this new society, reconciled through Christ to God and one another, are being drawn from all races and cultures. Indeed, this single new humanity—which Christ has created and in which no barriers are tolerated—is an essential part of the Good News (Eph 2:11-22). EVANGELISM AND SOCIAL RESPONSIBILITY, 1982

The calling of the church. We believe in one holy, universal, and apostolic Church. Its calling is to worship and witness concerning its Head, Jesus Christ, preaching the Gospel among all nations and demonstrating its commitment by compassionate service to the needs of human beings and promoting righteousness and justice. PRISON FELLOWSHIP MINISTRIES

The task of the church. We believe that the one, holy, universal Church is the body of Christ and is composed of the communities of Christ's people. The task of Christ's people in this world is to be God's redeemed community, embodying His love by worshiping God with confession, prayer, and praise; by proclaiming the gospel of God's redemptive love through our Lord Jesus Christ to the ends of the earth by word and deed; by caring for all of God's creation and actively seeking the good of everyone, especially the poor and needy. WHEATON COLLEGE

Fellowship in the body of Christ. God by his word and Spirit creates the one holy catholic and apostolic church, calling sinners out of the whole human race into the fellowship of Christ's body. By the same word and Spirit, he guides and preserves for eternity that new, redeemed humanity, which, being formed in every culture, is spiritually one with the people of God in all ages. FULLER THEOLOGICAL SEMINARY: STATEMENT OF FAITH

2. THE UNITY OF BELIEVERS

Members one of another. The Church is the universal body of Christ composed of all true believers in Christ, with Christ as its head (Col 1:18). All who are born again are baptized into this one Church by the Holy Spirit (1 Cor 12:12-13). Christ builds His own Church (Mt 16:18). This Church does not become fractured by the fact that there is more than one denomination, nor does it become one through church union; for there never can be more than one true body of Christ (Eph 4:4), and its membership record is in heaven, not on earth (Heb 12:23). All true Christians are members of one another (1 Cor 12:12-27; Eph 4:25). It is the responsibility of this Church and of each of its members to obey Christ's Great Commission to it and reach the whole world with the Gospel of Christ (Mt 28:18-20; Mk 16:15; Lk 24:47-49; Jn 20:21-22; Acts 1:8). OMS INTERNATIONAL

The unity of the Spirit. [We believe in] the unity of the Spirit of all true believers, the Church, the Body of Christ. WORLD EVANGELICAL ALLIANCE

The spiritual unity of believers. We believe in . . . the Spiritual Unity of all those who, having believed in Jesus Christ for their salvation, have been regenerated by the Holy Spirit and compose therefore the Church, the body of Christ of which He is the Head. EVANGELICAL ASSOCIATION OF THE CARIBBEAN

United in Christ. All believers in the Lord Jesus Christ are spiritually united with each other. They comprise the Church, the Body of Christ, of which He is the Head. EVANGELICAL SEMINARY OF SOUTH AFRICA

The redeemed of all ages. The church is the people of God, the body and the bride of Christ, and the temple of the Holy Spirit. The one, universal church is a transnational, transcultural, transdenominational and multi-ethnic family of the household of faith. In the widest sense, the church includes all the redeemed of all the ages, being the one body of Christ extended throughout time as well as space. AMSTERDAM DECLARATION, 2000, DEFINITIONS 9

One family. As Evangelicals united in the Gospel, we promise to watch over and care for one another, to pray for and forgive one another, and to reach out in love and truth to God's people everywhere, for we are one family, one in the Holy Spirit, and one in Christ. GOSPEL OF JESUS CHRIST, COMMITMENT

3. THE BODY OF CHRIST

The living body of Christ. We believe . . . that the Church consisting of all true believers, being Christ's own and indwelt by the Holy Spirit, is the body of Christ, the invisible Church; that the Church is holy, universal and one in Christ. CHINA GRADUATE SCHOOL OF THEOLOGY

The regenerated body. We believe that the true Church is composed of all such persons who through saving faith in Jesus Christ have been regenerated by the Holy Spirit and are united together in the body of Christ of which He is the Head. TRINITY EVANGELICAL DIVINITY SCHOOL

Formed by the Spirit. We believe that the true church which is the body of Christ (Eph 1:23), is formed by the work of the Holy Spirit in all those who trust Christ as their Savior (Eph 2:22; 1 Cor 12:13). HCJB WORLD RADIO/WORLD RADIO MISSIONARY FELLOWSHIP

4. CHRIST AND THE CHURCH

The head of the body. Jesus Christ is the Head of the Church, His Body, which is composed of all men, living and dead, who have been joined to Him through saving faith. CAMPUS CRUSADE FOR CHRIST

United by faith to Christ. We believe . . . that the Church is the body of Christ; that all who are united by faith to Christ are members of the same; and that, having thus become members one of another, it is our solemn and covenant duty to fellowship with one another in peace, and to love one another with pure and fervent hearts. WORLD GOSPEL MISSION

Submission to Christ. The Church is the Body of Christ. Christ is the head, and all born of the Holy Spirit are members of it. The Church on earth is to be in submission to Christ its head, maintain its faith and purity, obey His commands, and proclaim the gospel to all men. JAPAN BIBLE SEMINARY 8

The bride of Christ. We believe in the Church, the bride of Christ, comprising the whole body of those who have been born in the Spirit; and its local expression established for worship, mutual edification, and witness. NORTH AMERICAN INDIAN MINISTRIES

5. VISIBLE AND INVISIBLE, LOCAL AND GLOBAL

The invisible manifests itself in the visible. We believe . . . that the invisible Church manifests itself in the visible Church, the local congregations consisting of all who profess to believe in Christ and are baptized; that as the people of God and a kingdom of priests, the Church is called to grow unto the stature of the fullness of Christ and to fulfill her missionary task through the exercise of the gifts of the Holy Spirit, in worship, sacraments, fellowship, discipline, and service. CHINA GRADUATE SCHOOL OF THEOLOGY

The church becoming visible in the world. Here in the world, the church becomes visible in all local congregations that meet to do together the things that according to Scripture the church does. Christ is the head of the church. Everyone who is personally united to Christ by faith belongs to his body and by the Spirit is united with every other true believer in Jesus. AMSTERDAM DECLARATION, 2000, DEFINITIONS 9

***Defining* Christian.** A Christian is a believer in God who is enabled by the Holy Spirit to submit to Jesus Christ as Lord and Savior in a personal relationship of disciple to master and to live the life of God's kingdom. The word Christian should not be equated with any particular cultural, ethnic, political, or ideological tradition or group. Those who know and love Jesus are also called Christ-followers, believers and disciples. AMSTERDAM DECLARATION, 2000, DEFINITIONS 8

The church as local and global. A church which sends out missionaries must not neglect its own locality, and a church which evangelizes its neighborhood must not ignore the rest of the world.

In all this each congregation and denomination should, where possible, work with others, seeking to turn any spirit of competition into one of cooperation. Churches should also work with para-church organizations, especially in evangelism, discipling and community service, for such agencies are part of the Body of Christ, and have valuable, specialist expertise from which the church can greatly benefit. MANILA MANIFESTO, 1989, PART OF CLAUSE B.8

A world fellowship locally experienced.

We recognize the Church
as the body of Christ, of which he is the head,
held together and growing up in him through the one Spirit; both
as a total fellowship throughout the world, and
as local congregations in which believers gather to worship God,
growing in grace through Word, prayer and sacrament.

LONDON BIBLE COLLEGE

Visibly expressing the one universal church. The one universal church, the body of Christ, of which each local church is a visible expression, consists of all true believers born again by the Holy Spirit. As a fellowship of believers, the church is called to worship God, grow in grace and bear witness to Christ and His kingdom throughout the world. EUROPEAN CHRISTIAN MISSION INTERNATIONAL

6. THE FELLOWSHIP OF BELIEVERS

The human witnesses to God's good news. God the evangelist gives his people the privilege of being his "fellow workers." For, although we cannot witness without him, he normally chooses to witness through us. He calls only some to be evangelists, missionaries or pastors, but he calls his whole church and every member of it to be his witnesses. MANILA MANIFESTO, 1989, PART OF CLAUSE B.6

The priesthood of believers. We believe in the priesthood of all believers, who, together, constitute the universal church, the body of Christ, of which He is the head, and which, by His command, is called to worship and serve God in the world, to proclaim and defend His truth, to exhibit His character, and to demonstrate the reality of His kingdom through the local church and by their individual lifestyles. EVANGELICAL THEOLOGICAL FACULTY (EVANGELISCHE THEOLOGISCHE FACULTEIT, BELGIUM)

Lay witness. Lay witness takes place, by women and men, not only through the local church, . . . but through friendships, in the home and at work. Even those who are homeless or unemployed share in the calling to be witnesses. Our first responsibility is to witness to those who are already our friends, relatives, neighbors, and colleagues. . . . Work is a divine calling. Christians can commend Christ by word of mouth, by their consistent industry, honesty and thoughtfulness, by their concern for justice in the workplace, and especially if others can see from the quality of their daily work that it is done to the glory of God. MANILA MANIFESTO, 1989, PART OF CLAUSE B.6

7. THE WORSHIPING COMMUNITY

The worship of God. The church is summoned by Christ to offer acceptable worship to God and to serve him by preaching the gospel and making disciples of all nations, by tending the flock through the ministry of the word and sacraments and through daily pastoral care, by striving for social justice and by relieving human distress and need. FULLER THEOLOGICAL SEMINARY: STATEMENT OF FAITH

The privilege of assembling regularly for worship. God admonishes His people to assemble together regularly for worship, for participation in ordinances, for edification through the Scriptures and for mutual encouragement. CAMPUS CRUSADE FOR CHRIST

Worship and witness. Every Christian congregation is a local expression of the Body of Christ and has the same responsibilities. It is both "a holy priesthood" to offer God the spiritual sacrifices of worship and "a holy nation" to spread abroad his excellences in witness. The church is thus both a worshiping and a witnessing community gathered and scattered, called and sent. Worship and witness are inseparable. MANILA MANIFESTO, 1989, PART OF CLAUSE B.8

Proclamation requires decision. The appropriation of this salvation to individuals takes place first, however, through proclamation, which calls for decision, and through baptism, which places the believer in the service of love. FRANKFURT DECLARATION, 1970

8. OBSERVING GOD'S ORDINANCES

To glorify God. This universal Body of Christ is visibly expressed in local assemblies, whose purpose is to glorify God through worship, fellowship, instruction in God's Word, observing the ordinances and training in service to the world. BACK TO THE BIBLE

The Word preached, enacted and lived. The church is Christ's body; it is visible in the world wherever believers, in obedience of faith, hear the Word, receive the sacraments, and live as disciples. ASBURY THEOLOGICAL SEMINARY

Participating in his death and resurrection. We decry the poverty of sacramental understanding among Evangelicals. This is largely due to the loss of our continuity with the teaching of many of the Fathers and Reformers and results in the deterioration of sacramental life in our churches. Also, the failure to appreciate the sacramental nature of God's activity in the world often leads us to disregard the sacredness of daily living. Therefore we call Evangelicals to awaken to the sacramental implication of creation and incarnation. For in these doctrines the historic church has affirmed that God's activity is manifested in a material way. We need to recognize that the grace of God is mediated through faith by the operation of the Holy Spirit in a notable way in the sacraments of baptism and the Lord's Supper. Here the church proclaims, celebrates and participates in the death and resurrection of

Christ in such a way as to nourish her members throughout their lives in anticipation of the consummation of the kingdom. Also, we should remember our biblical designation as "living epistles," for here the sacramental character of the Christian's daily life is expressed. CHICAGO CALL, 1977

Dying and rising with Christ. All who repent and believe on Christ as Saviour and Lord are to be baptized. Thus they declare to the world that they died with Christ and that they also have been raised with Him to walk in newness of life (Mt 28:19; Mk 16:16; Acts 10:47, 48; Rom 6:4). INTERNATIONAL PENTECOSTAL CHURCH OF CHRIST

The Lord's Supper. The Lord's Supper, consisting of the elements—bread and fruit of the vine—is the symbol expressing our sharing the divine nature of our Lord Jesus Christ (2 Pet 1:4); a memorial of His suffering and death (1 Cor 11:26); and a prophecy of His second coming (1 Cor 11:26); and is enjoined on all believers "until He comes!" INTERNATIONAL PENTECOSTAL CHURCH OF CHRIST

9. CHURCH ORDER AND LEADERSHIP

Godly authority in the church. We deplore our disobedience to the Lordship of Christ as expressed through authority in his church. This has promoted a spirit of autonomy of persons and groups resulting in isolationism and competitiveness, even anarchy, within the body of Christ. We regret that in the absence of godly authority, there have risen legalistic, domineering leaders on the one hand and indifference to church discipline on the other. Therefore we affirm that all Christians are to be in practical submission to one another and to designated leaders in a church under the Lordship of Christ. The church, as the people of God, is called to be the visible presence of Christ in the world. CHICAGO CALL, 1977

Church order. We believe Christ authorized the ordination and appointment of men as pastors for the congregations, to expound the Word of God, to feed the flock, to serve as leaders, to administer the ordinances, to exercise scriptural church discipline, and to function as servant/leaders of the church. Ordination includes the setting apart for a particular responsibility by the church through the laying on of hands and the invocation of divine strength for the assignment. In the New Testament, the primary office was that of the apostle; others were gifted as prophets, evangelists, pastors, and teachers. The early church had regional overseers or bishops, such as Timothy, and pastors and deacons in the local congregations. These brethren were responsible for the leadership and pastoral care of the congregations and the maintenance of order in the church. We believe the New Testament provides us with the pattern of leadership for the continuing life of the church. A MENNONITE CONFESSION OF FAITH, 1990, ARTICLE 10

Worship and church discipline. Every Christian is called to active priesthood in worship and service through exercising spiritual gifts and ministries. In the church we are in vital union both with Christ and with one another. This calls for community with deep involvement and mutual commitment of time, energy and possessions. Further, church discipline, biblically based and under the direction of the Holy Spirit, is essential to the well-being and ministry of God's people. Moreover, we encourage all Christian organizations to conduct their activities with genuine accountability to the whole church. CHICAGO CALL, 1977

Leading the church in ministry. A divinely called and scripturally ordained ministry has been provided by our Lord for the threefold purpose of leading the Church in: (1) Evangelization of the world (Mk 16:15-20); (2) Worship of God (Jn 4:23, 24); (3) Building a body of saints being perfected in the image of His Son (Eph 4:11-16). INTERNATIONAL PENTECOSTAL CHURCH OF CHRIST

Spiritual care of the faithful. We are responsible to arrange for the spiritual care of those who come to faith under our ministry, to encourage them to identify with the local body of believers, and to seek to provide for the instruction of believers in witnessing to the Gospel. AMSTERDAM AFFIRMATIONS 1983

Discipling believers through proclamation. We affirm that Jesus Christ commands his followers to proclaim the Gospel to all living persons, evangelizing everyone everywhere, and discipling believers within the fellowship of the church. A full and faithful witness to Christ includes the witness of personal testimony, godly living, and acts of mercy and charity to our neighbor, without which the preaching of the Gospel appears barren. We deny that the witness of personal testimony, godly living, and acts of mercy and charity to our neighbors constitutes evangelism apart from the proclamation of the Gospel. GOSPEL OF JESUS CHRIST, AFFIRMATIONS AND DENIALS 18

10. RELIGIOUS FREEDOM

Freedom of religion for all. Christians earnestly desire freedom of religion for all people, not just freedom for Christianity. In predominantly Christian countries, Christians are at the forefront of those who demand freedom for religious minorities. In predominantly non-Christian countries, therefore, Christians are asking for themselves no more than they demand for others in similar circumstances. The freedom to "profess, practice and propagate" religion, as defined in the Universal Declaration of Human Rights, could and should surely be a reciprocally granted right.

We greatly regret any unworthy witness of which followers of Jesus may have been guilty. MANILA MANIFESTO, 1989, PART OF CLAUSE C.12

Seeking freedom for those unjustly imprisoned. It is the God-appointed duty of every government to secure conditions of peace, justice and liberty in which the church may obey God, serve the Lord Christ, and preach the gospel without interference. We therefore pray for the leaders of the nations and call upon them to guarantee freedom of thought and conscience, and freedom to practice and propagate religion in accordance with the will of God and as set forth in the Universal Declaration of Human Rights. We also express our deep concern for all who have been unjustly imprisoned, and especially for our brethren who are suffering for their testimony to the Lord Jesus. We promise to pray and work for their freedom. At the same time we refuse to be intimidated by their fate. God helping us, we too will seek to stand against injustice and to remain faithful to the gospel, whatever the cost. We do not forget the warnings of Jesus that persecution is inevitable. (1 Tim 1:1-4; Acts 4:19; 5:29; Col 3:24; Heb 13:1-3; Lk 4:18; Gal 5:11; 6:12; Mt 5:10-12; Jn 15:18-21). LAUSANNE COVENANT, 1974

11. THE PERSECUTED CHURCH

The fellowship of suffering. We affirm our solidarity with those who suffer for the gospel, and will seek to prepare ourselves for the same possibility. We will also work for religious and political freedom everywhere. MANILA MANIFESTO, 1989, TWENTY-ONE AFFIRMATIONS 20

The cross and suffering. As our Lord called us to take up our crosses, we remind the church of our Lord's teaching that suffering is a part of authentic Christian life. In an increasingly violent and unjust world with political and economic oppression, we commit to equip ourselves and others to suffer in missionary service and to serve the suffering church. IGUASSU AFFIRMATION, 1999, COMMITMENTS 10

Suffering for righteousness's sake. It was necessary for the King to suffer in order to enter into his glory. Indeed, he suffered for us, leaving us an example that we should follow in his steps (1 Pet 2:21). To suffer for the sake of righteousness or for our testimony to Jesus, and to bear such suffering courageously, is a clear sign to all beholders that we have received God's salvation or kingdom (Phil 1:28, 29; cf. 2 Thess 1:5). EVANGELISM AND SOCIAL RESPONSIBILITY, 1982

Transformation through patient suffering. There have been many occasions in the history of the church—and some exist today—where Christians, faced with persecution and oppression, have *appeared* to be disengaged from society and thus to support the status quo. We suggest, however, that even under conditions of the most severe repression, such Christians may in fact be challenging society and even be transforming it, through their lifestyles, their selfless love, their quiet joy, their inner peace, and their patient suffering (1 Pet 2:21-25). TRANSFORMATION: THE CHURCH IN RESPONSE TO HUMAN NEED, 1983

The persecuted church. Jesus plainly told his followers to expect opposition. "If they persecuted me," he said, "they will persecute you also." He even told them to rejoice over persecution, and reminded them that the condition of fruitfulness was death.

These predictions, that Christian suffering is inevitable and productive, have come true in every age, including our own. There have been many thousands of martyrs. Today the situation is much the same. . . .

Christians are loyal citizens, who seek the welfare of their nation. They pray for its leaders, and pay their taxes. Of course, those who have confessed Jesus as Lord cannot also call other authorities Lord, and if commanded to do so, or to do anything which God forbids, must disobey. But they are conscientious citizens. They also contribute to their country's well-being by the stability of their marriages and their homes, their honesty in business, their hard work and their voluntary activity in the service of the handicapped and needy. Just governments have nothing to fear from Christians. . . .

Christians renounce unworthy methods of evangelism. Though the nature of our faith requires us to share the gospel with others, our practice is to make an open and honest statement of it, which leaves the hearers entirely free to make up their own minds about it. We wish to be sensitive to those of other faiths, and we reject any approach that seeks to force conversion on them. . . .

We greatly regret any unworthy witness of which followers of Jesus may have been guilty. We determine to give no unnecessary offence in anything, lest the name of Christ be dishonored. However, the offence of the cross we cannot avoid. For the sake of Christ crucified we pray that we may be ready, by his grace, to suffer and even to die. Martyrdom is a form of witness which Christ has promised especially to honor. MANILA MANIFESTO , 1989, PART OF CLAUSE C.12

14

Religious Pluralism and the Uniqueness of Christ

Salvation in Christ Alone

Salvation is found in Christ alone. God witnesses to himself in creation and in human conscience, but these witnesses are not complete without the revelation of God in Christ. In the face of competing truth claims, we proclaim with humility that Christ is the only Savior, conscious that sin as well as cultural hindrances often mask him from those for whom he died.

IGUASSU AFFIRMATION, 1999, DECLARATIONS 2

1. The World Mission of the Church

The Father's sending of the Son, who sends the church to the world. Formed from *missio*, the Latin word for "sending," this term is used both of the Father's sending of the Son into the world to become its Savior and of the Son's sending the church into the world to spread the gospel, perform works of love and justice, and seek to disciple everyone to himself. AMSTERDAM DECLARATION, 2000, DEFINITIONS 10

Sent into the world. We affirm that Christ sends his redeemed people into the world as the Father sent him, and that this calls for a similar deep and costly penetration of the world. We need to break out of our ecclesiastical ghettos and permeate non-Christian society. In the church's mission of sacrificial service evangelism is primary. World evangelization requires the whole church to take the whole gospel to the whole world. The church is at the very center of God's cosmic purpose and is his appointed means of spreading the gospel. But a church which preaches the cross must itself be marked by the cross. It becomes a stumbling block to evangelism when it betrays the gospel or lacks a living faith in God, a genuine love for people, or scrupulous honesty in all things including promotion and finance. The church is the community of God's people rather than an institution, and must not be identified with any particular culture, social or political system, or human ideology. (Jn 17:18; 20:21; Mt 28:19, 20; Acts 1:8; 20:27; Eph 1:9, 10; 3:9-11; Gal 6:14, 17; 2 Cor 6:3, 4; 2 Tim 2:19-21; Phil 1:27). LAUSANNE COVENANT, 1974

Triune basis of mission. We do not exaggerate when we affirm that the living God is a missionary God. He created all humankind, is "the God of the spirits of all flesh," and when calling Abraham promised through his posterity to bless "all the families of the earth." Next, Jesus Christ during his public ministry sent his disciples to "the lost sheep of the house of Israel," and subsequently he commissioned them to go and make disciples of all the nations. Between these two missions lay his death and resurrection. He died on the cross for the sins of the world, and was raised and exalted to be Lord. The church's universal mission derives from Christ's universal authority. Thirdly, the Holy Spirit is a missionary Spirit, and Pentecost was a missionary event. He gave his people power for witness, as Jesus promised, and thrust them out to the ends of the earth, as Jesus foretold (Acts 1:8). This Trinitarian basis for mission is primary. It is the missionary heart of God himself, Father, Son and Holy Spirit. If he yearns in his love for his lost world, we his people must share his yearning. Commitment to world mission is unavoidable, and indifference to it inexcusable. EVANGELISM AND SOCIAL RESPONSIBILITY, 1982

The presence of the kingdom. "The time has come," Jesus announced as he began his public ministry, "the kingdom of God is near. Repent and believe the Good News" (Mk 1:15). Thus Jesus brought the kingdom with him. "Eschatology invaded history." "The person of Jesus and the presence of God's kingdom are inseparably connected." Only those enter it who humble themselves like a little child and are born again. The kingdom of God is both a present reality and a future expectation. As a present reality, now that Jesus' physical presence has been withdrawn from the earth, his Holy Spirit establishes it in the lives of his people. For the King must never be thought of apart from his subjects, the messianic community, over which he rules. Moreover, his rule takes the form of both total blessing (salvation, in fact) and total demand (obedience and service). EVANGELISM AND SOCIAL RESPONSIBILITY, 1982, 5B

The mission of the church. We affirm that the mission of the church is to spread the good news of salvation by word and deed to a lost and despairing humanity. This mission to proclaim the atoning death and resurrection of Jesus Christ to all nations calls people of faith to discipleship and obedience in the pursuit of personal and social holiness. We further affirm that the fruit of the gospel proclamation is justice, mercy and peace. We deny that the mission of the church is the self-development of exploited peoples or the political liberation of oppressed peoples. DUPAGE DECLARATION, 1990

2. THE GREAT COMMISSION

To every nation. The Lord Jesus Christ commanded all believers to proclaim the Gospel throughout the world and to disciple men of every nation. The fulfillment of that Great Commission requires that all worldly and personal ambitions be subordinated to a total commitment to "Him who loved us and gave Himself for us." CAMPUS CRUSADE FOR CHRIST

Proclaiming, discipling, baptizing, teaching.

We acknowledge the commission of Christ
to proclaim the Good News to all people,
making them disciples, baptising them, and
teaching them to obey him.
We acknowledge the command of Christ
to love our neighbours,

resulting in service to the Church and to society,
in seeking reconciliation for all with God and their fellows,
in proclaiming liberty from every kind of oppression; and
in spreading Christ's justice in an unjust world.
LONDON BIBLE COLLEGE

Proclaim, invite, baptize, teach. Our Lord Jesus Christ, possessor of all authority in heaven and on earth, has not only called us to Himself; He has sent us out into the world to be His witnesses. In the power of His Spirit He commands us to proclaim to all people the good news of salvation through His atoning death and resurrection; to invite them to discipleship through repentance and faith; to baptize them into the fellowship of His Church; and to teach them all His words. BERLIN STATEMENT, 1966 (WORLD CONGRESS ON EVANGELISM, BERLIN, 1966)

The urgency of the Great Commission. In view of Christ's last command (Mt 28:19, 20) and recognizing the lost condition of all those who fail to accept the gospel message (Jn 3:18, 36), we believe in the urgency of every Christian's responding to the great commission of Christ. . . . It is to the work of helping to carry out the plan of God in this age that [we are] dedicated in conformity with the last command of our Savior to "be my witnesses . . . to the end of the earth" (Acts 1:8). With the God-given means at our disposal, the message of the gospel, which "is the power of God for the salvation of everyone who believes" (Rom 1:16), is being literally carried to the ends of the earth. We also seek to carry out the command of our Savior to teach all nations (Mt 18:20), in addition to evangelizing them. HCJB WORLD RADIO/WORLD RADIO MISSIONARY FELLOWSHIP

The time of mission. We believe that the interim period between Christ's ascension and return is to be filled with the mission of the people of God, who have no liberty to stop before the End. We also remember his warning that false Christs and false prophets will arise as precursors of the final Antichrist. We therefore reject as a proud, self-confident dream the notion that man can ever build a utopia on earth. Our Christian confidence is that God will perfect his kingdom, and we look forward with eager anticipation to that day, and to the new heaven and earth in which righteousness will dwell and God will reign for ever. Meanwhile, we rededicate ourselves to the service of Christ and of men and women in joyful submission to his authority over the whole of our lives. (Mk 14:62; Heb 9:28; Mk 13:10; Acts 1:8-11; Mt 28:20; Mk 13:21-23; Jn 2:18; 4:1-3; Lk 12:32; Rev 21:1-5; 2 Pet 3:13; Mt 28:18). LAUSANNE COVENANT, 1974, PART OF CLAUSE 15

The goal of history. Despite the difficulties, we look expectantly to the day when the Gospel finally "will be preached in all the world" (Mt 24:14), and the redeemed of the Lord will be gathered from "every tribe, and language, and people, and nation" to praise Him forever (Rev 5:9; 7:9). Our commitment to world evangelization directs our energy toward this goal to which history is moving, when the completed church will be presented to the Father in all the beauty of His holiness, and every knee shall bow and every tongue declare that Jesus Christ is Lord, to the glory of God (Phil 2:10-11; Rom 10:9-10; 1 Cor 12:3). GCOWE '95 (GLOBAL CONSULTATION ON WORLD EVANGELIZATION, SEOUL, 1995) DECLARATION —AD 2000 & BEYOND MOVEMENT

3. THE WHOLE GOSPEL FOR THE WHOLE WORLD

Establishing healthy, reproducing, indigenous churches. The mission of the church has at its heart world evangelization. We have from our Lord a mandate to proclaim the good news of God's love and forgiveness to everyone, making disciples, baptizing, and teaching all peoples. Jesus made it clear in his last teachings that the scope of this work of evangelism demands that we give attention not only to those around us but also to the despised and neglected of society and to those at the ends of the earth. To do anything less is disobedience. In addition, we affirm the need to encourage new initiatives to reach and disciple youth and children worldwide; to make fuller use of media and technology in evangelism; and to stay involved personally in grass-roots evangelism so that our presentations of the biblical gospel are fully relevant and contextualized. We think it urgent to work toward the evangelization of every remaining unreached people group.

We pledge ourselves to work so that all persons on earth may have the opportunity to hear the gospel in a language they understand, near where they live. We further pledge to establish healthy, reproducing, indigenous churches among every people, in every place, that will seek to bring to spiritual maturity those who respond to the gospel message. AMSTERDAM DECLARATION, 2000, CHARTER 1

The whole church for the whole world. We affirm that God is calling the whole church to take the whole gospel to the whole world. So we determine to proclaim it faithfully, urgently and sacrificially until he comes. MANILA MANIFESTO, 1989, TWENTY-ONE AFFIRMATIONS 21

Understanding the world into which we are sent. The whole gospel has been entrusted to the whole church, in order that it may be made known to the whole world. It is necessary, therefore, for us to understand the world into which we are sent. MANILA MANIFESTO, 1989

Preaching the gospel to all. We affirm that the church is commanded by God and is therefore under divine obligation to preach the Gospel to every living person (Lk 24:47; Mt 28:18-19). We deny that any particular class or group of persons, whatever their ethnic or cultural identity, may be ignored or passed over in the preaching of the Gospel (1 Cor 9:19-22). God purposes a global church made up from people of every tribe, language, and nation (Rev 7:9). GOSPEL OF JESUS CHRIST, AFFIRMATIONS AND DENIALS 5

The mandate. The Church is given the mandate by the Risen Lord Jesus and is under obligation to demonstrate and proclaim the wholeness of the Gospel and its implications to the whole creation. SOUTH ASIA INSTITUTE OF ADVANCED CHRISTIAN STUDIES

Accepting the call. We affirm our commitment to the Great Commission of our Lord, and we declare our willingness to go anywhere, do anything, and sacrifice anything God requires of us in the fulfillment of that Commission. We respond to God's call to the biblical ministry of the evangelist, and accept our solemn responsibility to preach the Word to all peoples as God gives opportunity. AMSTERDAM AFFIRMATIONS 1983

The outpouring of sovereign grace. We yearn for an outpouring of sovereign grace and power in a mighty spiritual awakening across the length and breadth of the church. The magnitude of this task is beyond our resources, but we know that with God all things are possible (2 Cor 10:4; Lk 1:37; Phil 4:13). GCOWE '95 (GLOBAL CONSULTATION ON WORLD EVANGELIZATION, SEOUL, 1995) DECLARATION —AD 2000 & BEYOND MOVEMENT

4. THE MODERN WORLD

The modern world. Evangelism takes place in a context, not in a vacuum. The balance between gospel and context must be carefully maintained. We must understand the context in order to address it, but the context must not be allowed to distort the gospel.

In this connection we have become concerned about the impact of "modernity," which is an emerging world culture produced by industrialization with its technology and urbanization with its economic order. These factors combine to create an environment, which significantly shapes the way in which we see our world. In addition, secularism has devastated faith by making God and the supernatural meaningless; urbanization has dehumanized life for many; and the mass media have contributed to the devaluation of truth and authority, by replacing word with image. In combination, these consequences of modernity pervert the message which many preach and undermine their motivation for mission. MANILA MANIFESTO, 1989, PART OF CLAUSE C.10

The advantages and disadvantages of modernization. Modernization brings blessings as well as dangers. By creating links of communication and commerce around the globe, it makes unprecedented openings for the gospel, crossing old frontiers and penetrating closed societies, whether traditional or totalitarian. MANILA MANIFESTO, 1989, PART OF CLAUSE C.10

Use of modern means. [We believe] in using every modern means of communication available to us to spread the Gospel of Jesus Christ throughout the world. BILLY GRAHAM EVANGELISTIC ASSOCIATION

The neglected. More than 2,700 million people, which is more than two-thirds of mankind, have yet to be evangelized. We are ashamed that so many have been neglected; it is a standing rebuke to us and to the whole church. There is now, however, in many parts of the world an unprecedented receptivity to the Lord Jesus Christ. We are convinced that this is the time for churches and para-church agencies to pray earnestly for the salvation of the unreached and to launch new efforts to achieve world evangelization. . . . The goal should be, by all available means and at the earliest possible time, that every person will have the opportunity to hear, understand, and receive the good news. We cannot hope to attain this goal without sacrifice. LAUSANNE COVENANT, 1974, PART OF CLAUSE 9

The unreached. Our primary but not exclusive focus is on the "10/40 Window" (the area of ten to forty degrees North of the equator from West Africa to East Asia) where most of the unreached people groups are located. There also we find the greatest degrees of poverty, illiteracy, disease and suffering. GCOWE'95 (GLOBAL CONSULTATION ON WORLD EVANGELIZATION, SEOUL, 1995) DECLARATION—AD 2000 & BEYOND MOVEMENT

5. THE UNIQUENESS OF JESUS CHRIST AND RELIGIOUS PLURALISM

Religious pluralism. Today's evangelist is called to proclaim the gospel in an increasingly pluralistic world. In this global village of competing faiths and many world religions, it is important that our evangelism be marked both by faithfulness to the good news of Christ and humility in our delivery of it. Because God's general revelation extends to all points of his creation, there may well be traces of truth, beauty and goodness in many non-Christian belief systems. But we have no warrant for regarding any of these as alternative gospels or separate roads to salvation. The only way to know God in peace, love and joy is through the reconciling death of Jesus Christ the risen Lord. As we share this message with others, we must do so with love and humility shunning all arrogance, hostility and disrespect. As we enter into dialogue with adherents of other religions, we must be courteous and kind. But such dialogue must not be a substitute for proclamation. Yet because all persons are made in the image of God, we must advocate religious liberty and human rights for all.

We pledge ourselves to treat those of other faiths with respect and faithfully and humbly serve the nation in which God has placed us, while affirming that Christ is the one and only Savior of the world. AMSTERDAM DECLARATION, 2000, CHARTER 6

Addressing all human cultures. Culture must always be tested and judged by Scripture. Because man is God's creature, some of his culture is rich in beauty and goodness. Because he has fallen, all of it is tainted with sin and some of it is demonic. The gospel does not presuppose the superiority of any culture to another, but evaluates all cultures according to its own criteria of truth and righteousness, and insists on moral absolutes in every culture. Missions have all too frequently exported with the gospel an alien culture, and churches have sometimes been in bondage to culture rather than to the Scripture. Christ's evangelists must humbly seek to empty themselves of all but their personal authenticity in order to become the servants of others, and churches must seek to transform and enrich culture, all for the glory of God. (Mk 7:8, 9, 13; Gen 4:21, 22; 1 Cor 9:19-23; Phil 2:5-7; 2 Cor 4:5). LAUSANNE COVENANT, 1974, PART OF CLAUSE 10

Saints from every tribe and nation. By the blood of the Lamb, God has purchased saints from every tribe and language and people and nation. He saves people in their own culture. World evangelization aims to see the rise of churches that are both deeply rooted in Christ and closely related to their culture. Therefore, following the example of Jesus and Paul, those who proclaim Christ must use their freedom in Christ to become all things to all people. This means appropriate cultural identification while guarding against equating the gospel with any particular culture. Since all human cultures are shaped in part by sin, the Bible and its Christ are at key points counter-cultural to everyone of them. AMSTERDAM DECLARATION, 2000, CHARTER 7

Transcending barriers. We affirm that we who claim to be members of the Body of Christ must transcend within our fellowship the barriers of race, gender and class. MANILA MANIFESTO, 1989, TWENTY-ONE AFFIR-

MATIONS 13

Overcoming cultural prejudices. We confess that our interpretation of Scripture has often been distorted by our cultural prejudices. We resolve to engage in cross-cultural biblical study, so that "with all God's people" we may grasp the dimensions of Christ's love. LIVING WORD FOR A DYING WORLD COMMON COMMITMENT , 1994

6. THE ONLY SAVIOR

The centrality of Jesus Christ. We are called to proclaim Christ in an increasingly pluralistic world. There is a resurgence of old faiths and a rise of new ones. In the first century too there were "many gods and many lords." Yet the apostles boldly affirmed the uniqueness, indispensability and centrality of Christ. We must do the same. MANILA MANIFESTO , 1989, PART OF CLAUSE A.3

Amid diverse religious aspirations. We proclaim the living Christ in a world torn by ethnic conflicts, massive economic disparity, natural disasters, and ecological crises. The mission task is both assisted and hindered by technological developments that now reach the remotest corners of the earth. The diverse religious aspirations of people, expressed in multiple religions and spiritual experimentation, challenge the ultimate truth of the gospel. IGUASSU AFFIRMATION , 1999, PREAMBLE

Religious people in need of redemption. Because men and women are made in God's image and see in the creation traces of its Creator, the religions which have arisen do sometimes contain elements of truth and beauty. They are not, however, alternative gospels. Because human beings are sinful, and because "the whole world is under the control of the evil one," even religious people are in need of Christ's redemption. We, therefore, have no warrant for saying that salvation can be found outside Christ or apart from an explicit acceptance of his work through faith. MANILA MANIFESTO , 1989, PART OF CLAUSE A.3

One gospel only. There is only one gospel because there is only one Christ, who because of his death and resurrection is himself the only way of salvation. We therefore reject both the relativism which regards all religions and spiritualities as equally valid approaches to God, and the syncretism which tries to mix faith in Christ with other faiths. MANILA MANIFESTO, 1989, PART OF CLAUSE A.3

Christ as the only way. We affirm that other religions and ideologies are not alternative paths to God, and that human spirituality, if unredeemed by Christ, leads not to God but to judgment, for Christ is the only way. MANILA MANIFESTO, 1989, TWENTY-ONE AFFIRMATIONS 7

Witness and interfaith dialogue. In the past we have sometimes been guilty of adopting towards adherents of other faiths attitudes of ignorance, arrogance, disrespect and even hostility. We repent of this. We nevertheless are determined to bear a positive and uncompromising witness to the uniqueness of our Lord, in his life, death and resurrection, in all aspects of our evangelistic work including inter-faith dialogue. MANILA MANIFESTO, 1989, PART OF CLAUSE A.3

Substitutes for proclamation. We refute the idea that "Christian presence" among the adherents to the world religions and give-and-take dialogue with them are substitutes for a proclamation of the Gospel which aims at conversion. FRANKFURT DECLARATION, 1970

The lordship of Christ. The kingdom of God is his gracious rule through Jesus Christ over human lives, the course of history, and all reality. Jesus is Lord of past, present, and future, and Sovereign ruler of everything. The salvation Jesus brings and the community of faith he calls forth are signs of his kingdom's presence here and now, though we wait for its complete fulfillment when he comes again in glory. In the meantime, wherever Christ's standards of peace and justice are observed to any degree, to that degree the kingdom is anticipated, and to that extent God's ideal for human society is displayed. AMSTERDAM DECLARATION, 2000, DEFINITIONS 5

7. THE GOSPEL AND THE JEWISH PEOPLE

The gospel and the Jews. We believe that Israel exists as a covenant people through whom God continues to accomplish His purposes and that the Church is an elect people in accordance with the New Covenant, comprising both Jews and Gentiles who acknowledge Jesus as Messiah and Redeemer. JEWS FOR JESUS

Election of Israel. We believe that God made an everlasting and irrevocable covenant with Abraham. CHOSEN PEOPLE MINISTRIES

Israel's vocation. First, God has used the Jewish people to give the Christian the way of salvation. Secondly, the Jewish people have a prior and continuing covenant relationship with God (Jer 31:31 ff.; Is 49:6). Part of that covenanted responsibility involves their being a light to the world. Jews, however, cannot perfectly fulfill that responsibility without Christ. Thirdly, Paul anticipated the turning of Jews to Christ which would have a life-giving impact on the entire church. CHRISTIAN WITNESS TO THE JEWISH PEOPLE, 1980

God did not reject his people. There is an attitude among many Christians that the Jews as a people no longer have a part in God's plan since Israel's prerogatives have passed *in toto* to the church. However, God called Abraham from among the nations and established a universal covenant with the patriarch and his seed to be a blessing to all peoples (Gen 12:1-3). This promise includes the preservation of Israel to carry out God's purpose, which was reaffirmed by Jeremiah (31:35-37). Paul echoes the promise in Romans 11:1, "Did God reject his people? By no means," and again in Romans 11:28 ". . . but as far as election is concerned, they are loved on account of the patriarchs." God has therefore preserved Israel according to the flesh and he is not yet finished with the Jewish people in his redemptive plan for mankind. CHRISTIAN WITNESS TO THE JEWISH PEOPLE, 1980

Fellow heirs. We believe that the church is comprised of both Jews and Gentiles who have accepted Jesus as Messiah. Gentiles who have come to faith in Messiah Jesus are fellow heirs with Jewish believers of the promises of God. We believe in the establishment of the local assembly of believers where both Jews and Gentiles are encouraged to live together in unity while expressing their respective cultural distinctives. CHOSEN PEOPLE MINISTRIES

Who is a Jew? In contemporary Jewish thinking, a Jew is considered to be anyone who has some Jewish origin by birth or who has undergone conversion. According to Jewish Orthodox law, a Jew is one born of a Jewish mother. For us, the definition of a Jew is a person who belongs to the people with whom God made certain immutable and eternal covenants. CHRISTIAN WITNESS TO THE JEWISH PEOPLE, 1980

Converted Jews remain Jews. The Jew who is brought to faith in Christ does not cease being a Jew. Therefore, although he has the freedom in Christ to conform to common patterns of piety and religious observances practiced by all Christians, he must be accorded the freedom in Christ to observe religious elements appropriate to him as an Israelite (e.g., Jewish religious festivals) so long as they are kept in a manner consistent with the Scripture. CHRISTIAN WITNESS TO THE JEWISH PEOPLE, 1980

8. RELATIONS BETWEEN JEWS AND CHRISTIANS

Indifference unjustified. We affirm that Jewish people have an ongoing part in God's plan. We deny that indifference to the future of the Jewish people on the part of Christians can ever be justified. WILLOWBANK DECLARATION, 1989, 3.12

Obstacles to communication. There are many obstacles to the communication of the gospel to the Jewish people. Some of these communication blocks arise when Christians fail to take into account the uniqueness of the Jewish people, or fail to appreciate the harm done to the Jewish people by some who have called themselves Christians. On the other hand, it must be recognized that, as a defensive measure to preserve the Jewish people, Jewish leaders have set obstacles, both intellectual and social, to prevent Jews from considering the claims of Christ. CHRISTIAN WITNESS TO THE JEWISH PEOPLE, 1980

Shared scriptural accountability. The New Testament must therefore be held together with the Old and understood and interpreted on the background of the Old Testament Scriptures in study, worship, preaching, and witnessing. We make this call to the church not only to enhance the ability of the church to communicate the original Jewishness of Christianity to the Jewish people, but also because it is the Word of this one Bible that gives the church its identity, its mandate in the world, and its power to serve. CHRISTIAN WITNESS TO THE JEWISH PEOPLE, 1980

Adherence to triune teaching. While we adhere to the formulation of the doctrine on the Trinity in the creeds of the early church councils, we feel that it is essential to present our faith in the one God—Father, Son, and Holy Spirit—in biblical terms, making use of the rich material found in both Testaments as well as in the intertestamental literature. CHRISTIAN WITNESS TO THE JEWISH PEOPLE, 1980

9. REPENTING OF ANTI-SEMITISM

Our whole race sent Christ to the cross. We affirm that it was the sins of the whole human race that sent Christ to the cross. We deny that it is right to single out the Jewish people for putting Jesus to death. WILLOWBANK DECLARATION, 1989, 3.18

Historical anti-Semitism and present relations. We affirm that anti-Semitism on the part of professed Christians has always been wicked and shameful and that the church has in the past been much to blame for tolerating and encouraging it and for condoning anti-Jewish actions on the part of individuals and governments. We deny that these past failures, for which offending Gentile believers must ask forgiveness from both God and the Jewish community, rob Christians of the right or lessen their responsibility to share the Gospel with Jews today and for the future. WILLOWBANK DECLARATION, 1989, 3.17

10. THE GIFTS OF JEWS TO CHRISTIANS

Christian indebtedness to the Jewish people. Every Christian must acknowledge an immense debt of gratitude to the Jewish people. The Gospel is the good news that Jesus is the Christ, the long-promised Jewish Messiah, who by his life, death and resurrection saves from sin and all its consequences. Those who worship Jesus as their Divine Lord and Savior have thus received God's most precious gift through the Jewish people. Therefore they have compelling reason to show love to that people in every possible way. Concerned about humanity everywhere, we are resolved to uphold the right of Jewish people to a just and peaceful existence everywhere, both in the land of Israel and in their communities throughout the world. We repudiate past persecutions of Jews by those identified as Christians, and we pledge ourselves to resist every form of anti-Semitism. WILLOWBANK DECLARATION, 1989, PREAMBLE

Christian roots in Jewish history. We deny that Christian faith is necessarily non-Jewish, and that Gentiles who believe in Christ may ignore their solidarity with believing Jews, or formulate their new identity in Christ without reference to Jewishness, or decline to receive the Hebrew Scriptures as part of their own instruction from God, or refuse to see themselves as having their roots in Jewish history. We affirm that Jewish people who come to faith in Messiah have liberty before God to observe or not observe traditional Jewish customs and ceremonies that are consistent with the Christian Scriptures and do not hinder fellowship with the rest of the Body of Christ. WILLOWBANK DECLARATION, 1989, 2.10-11

The rich heritage. Christians must be aware of their indebtedness to Jewish people through whom God has committed to the church a rich heritage including both the Savior and the Scriptures. The liturgical riches of prayer, psalmody, and the Law, as well as the use of symbols which relate to the Jewish tradition, can appropriately be incorporated into worship. CHRISTIAN WITNESS TO THE JEWISH PEOPLE, 1980

Commending those who risk death for Jews. We urge Christians to follow the example of those ministers of the church who, through heroic acts, have given themselves to work for the welfare and preservation of the Jewish people even to the point of risking death. CHRISTIAN WITNESS TO THE JEWISH PEOPLE, 1980

11. GRACE AND LAW

Resisting antinomianism. As we approach Jews it is very important for them to see that we are saved by grace alone, but also that life in Christ is lived in accordance with the holy will of God. We therefore call upon the church to reject antinomian tendencies, and particularly to give new emphasis in its instruction of believers to do the will of God as revealed in the

Old Testament. CHRISTIAN WITNESS TO THE JEWISH PEOPLE, 1980

The Law not abolished, but fulfilled. Whereas modern Judaism can describe the Law and the commandments as the ladder on which man shall climb up to God, the New Testament proclaims that we are all sinners, condemned by his holy Law and unable to reach up to him through any manner of works. There is only one way, Jesus Christ, who came down from heaven and has given us access to the Father through himself. However, Jesus also strongly states that he did not come to abolish the Law. The Law still contains the revelation of the perfect will of God, and the new life in Christ is meant to be lived in full accordance with this will. CHRISTIAN WITNESS TO THE JEWISH PEOPLE, 1980

The cross and God's covenant with Israel. We affirm that prior to the coming of Christ it was Israel's unique privilege to enjoy a corporate covenantal relationship with God, following upon the national redemption from slavery, and involving God's gift of the law and of a theocratic culture; God's promise of blessing to faithful obedience; and God's provision of atonement for transgression. We affirm that within this covenant relationship, God's pardon and acceptance of the penitent which was linked to the offering of prescribed sacrifices rested upon the foreordained sacrifice of Jesus Christ. WILLOWBANK DECLARATION, 1989, 3.13

12. FUTURE FULFILLMENT

All Israel will be saved. While a part of Israel continues to reject God's Messiah, yet it is God's will that the church reach the remnant of Israel in every generation until the day when "all Israel will be saved." (Rom 11:26). CHRISTIAN WITNESS TO THE JEWISH PEOPLE, 1980

Regathering the branches. We therefore call upon the church to labor for the re-gathering of these natural branches into the olive tree, the covenantal fellowship with God in the Messiah, through faith in Christ and through the seal of the new covenant, which is baptism. We encourage the church to look forward to the day when we are again united with this Israel in the body of Christ, and when we together with Christ and one another will celebrate the meaning of the new covenant both here and in the eternal kingdom of God. CHRISTIAN WITNESS TO THE JEWISH PEOPLE, 1980

Prophecies fulfilled. We affirm that the God-given types, prophecies and visions of salvation and shalom in the Hebrew Scriptures find their present and future fulfillment in and through Jesus Christ, the Son of God, who by incarnation became a Jew and was shown to be the Son of God and Messiah by his resurrection. We deny that it is right to look for a Messiah who has not yet appeared in world history. WILLOWBANK DECLARATION, 1989, 1.2

15

Christian Social Responsibility

The Integration of Words and Deeds

The authentic gospel must become visible in the transformed lives of men and women. As we proclaim the love of God we must be involved in loving service; as we preach the Kingdom of God we must be committed to its demands of justice and peace.

Evangelism is primary because our chief concern is with the gospel, that all people may have the opportunity to accept Jesus Christ as Lord and Savior. Yet Jesus not only proclaimed the Kingdom of God, he also demonstrated its arrival by works of mercy and power. We are called today to a similar integration of words and deeds. In a spirit of humility we are to preach and teach, minister to the sick, feed the hungry, care for prisoners, help the disadvantaged and handicapped, and deliver the oppressed. While we acknowledge the diversity of spiritual gifts, callings and contexts, we also affirm that good news and good works are inseparable.

MANILA MANIFESTO, 1989,
PART OF CLAUSE A.4

1. Personal Salvation and Social Justice

Social suffering. We share Christ's deep concern for the personal and social sufferings of humanity, and we accept our responsibility as Christians and as evangelists to do our utmost to alleviate human need.
AMSTERDAM AFFIRMATIONS 1983

Personal and social responsibilities. Here too we express penitence both for our neglect and for having sometimes regarded evangelism and social concern as mutually exclusive. Although reconciliation with man is not reconciliation with God, nor is social action evangelism, nor is political liberation salvation, nevertheless we affirm that evangelism and socio-political involvement are both part of our Christian duty. For both are necessary expressions of our doctrines of God and man, our love for our neighbour and our obedience to Jesus Christ. The message of salvation implies also a message of judgment upon every form of alienation, oppression and discrimination, and we should not be afraid to denounce evil and injustice wherever they exist. When people receive Christ they are born again into his kingdom and must seek not only to exhibit but also to spread its righteousness in the midst of an unrighteous world. The salvation we claim should be transforming us in the totality of our personal and social responsibilities. Faith without works is dead. (Acts 17:26, 31; Gen 18:25; Is 1:17; Ps 45:7; Gen 1:26, 27; Jas 3:9; Lev 19:18; Lk 6:27, 35; Jas 2:14-26; Jn 3:3, 5; Mt 5:20; 6:33; 2 Cor 3:18; Jas 2:20). LAUSANNE COVENANT, 1974, PART OF CLAUSE 5

The social implications of the gospel. Our continuing commitment to social action is not a confusion of the kingdom of God with a Christianized society. It is, rather, a recognition that the biblical gospel has inescapable social implications. True mission should always be incarnational. It necessitates entering humbly into other people's worlds, identifying with their social reality, their sorrow and suffering, and their struggles for justice against oppressive powers. This cannot be done without personal sacrifices. MANILA MANIFESTO, 1989, PART OF CLAUSE A.4

Personal salvation and social justice. We deplore the tendency of Evangelicals to understand salvation solely as an individual, spiritual and otherworldly matter to the neglect of the corporate, physical and this-worldly implication of God's saving activity. Therefore we urge Evangelicals to recapture a holistic view of salvation. The witness of Scripture is that because of sin our relationships with God, ourselves, others and creation are broken. Through the atoning work of Christ on the cross, healing is possible for these broken relationships. Wherever the church has been faithful to its calling, it has proclaimed personal salvation; it has been a channel of God's healing to those in physical and emotional need; it has sought justice for the oppressed and disinherited; and it has been a good steward of the natural world. CHICAGO CALL, 1977

The servant spirit. We proclaim together, "Jesus lived, died and rose again. Jesus is Lord." We desire him to be central in our individual and corporate lives. We seek to follow him in his identification with the poor, the afflicted, the oppressed, the marginalized; in his special concern for children; in his respect for the dignity bestowed by God on women equally with men; in his challenge to unjust attitudes and systems; in his call to share resources with each other; in his love for all people without discrimination or conditions; in his offer of new life through faith in him. From him we derive our holistic understanding of the Gospel of the Kingdom of God, which forms the basis of our response to human need. We hear his call to servanthood and see the example of his life. We commit ourselves to a servant spirit permeating the organization. We know this means facing honestly our own pride, sin and failure. We bear witness to the redemption offered through faith in Jesus Christ. The staff we engage are equipped by belief and practice to bear this witness. We will maintain our identity as Christian, while being sensitive to the diverse contexts in which we express that identity. WORLD VISION

Resisting utopian captivity. We refute the identification of messianic salvation with progress, development, and social change. The fatal consequence of this is that efforts to aid development and revolutionary involvement in the places of tension in society are seen as the contemporary forms of Christian mission. But such an identification would be a self-deliverance to the utopian movements of our time in the direction of their ultimate destination. FRANKFURT DECLARATION , 1970

The tension between hope and realism. Some, inspired by a utopian vision, seem to suggest that God's Kingdom, in all its fullness, can be built on earth. We do not subscribe to this view, since Scripture informs us of the reality and pervasiveness of both personal and societal sin (Is 1:10-26; Amos 2:6-8; Mic 2:1-10; Rom 1:28-32). Thus we recognize that utopianism is nothing but a false dream. Other Christians become pessimistic because they are faced with the reality of increasing poverty and misery, of rampant oppression and exploitation by powers of the right and the left, of spiraling violence coupled with the threat of nuclear warfare. They are concerned, too, about the increasing possibility that planet earth will not be able to sustain its population for long because of the wanton squandering of its resources. As a result, they are tempted to turn their eyes away from this world and fix them so exclusively on the return of Christ that their involvement in the here and now is paralyzed. TRANSFORMATION : THE CHURCH IN RESPONSE TO HUMAN NEED, 1983

2. CARE FOR THE POOR

Caring for those deprived. We must demonstrate God's love visibly by caring for those who are deprived of justice, dignity, food and shelter. MANILA MANIFESTO, 1989, TWENTY-ONE AFFIRMATIONS 8

Good news for the poor. We have again been confronted with Luke's emphasis that the gospel is good news for the poor and have asked ourselves what this means to the majority of the world's population who are destitute, suffering or oppressed. We have been reminded that the law, the prophets and the wisdom books, all the teaching and ministry of Jesus, all stress God's concern for the materially poor and our consequent duty to defend and care for them. Scripture also refers to the spiritually poor who look to God alone for mercy. The gospel comes as good news to both. The spiritually poor, who, whatever their economic circumstances, humble themselves before God, receive by faith the free gift of salvation. There is no other way for anybody to enter the Kingdom of God. MANILA MANIFESTO, 1989, PART OF CLAUSE A.2

Commitment to the poor. We are committed to the poor. We are called specifically to serve the neediest people of the earth; to relieve their suffering and promote the transformation of their condition of life. We seek to understand the situation of the poor and work alongside them toward fullness of life. . . . We seek to facilitate an engagement between the poor and the affluent that opens both to transformation. We respect the poor as active participants, not passive recipients, in this relationship. WORLD VISION

The wretched of the earth. We are appalled to know that about 800 million people, or one-fifth of the human race, are destitute, lacking the basic necessities for survival, and that thousands of them die of starvation every day. Many more millions are without adequate shelter and clothing, without clean water and health care, without opportunities for education and employment, and are condemned to eke out a miserable existence without the possibility of self-improvement for themselves or their families. They can only be described as "oppressed" by the gross economic inequality from which they suffer and the diverse economic systems which cause and perpetuate it. The oppression of others is political. They are denied fundamental human rights by totalitarian regimes of the extreme left or right, while if they protest they are imprisoned without trial, tortured, and killed. EVANGELISM AND SOCIAL RESPONSIBILITY, 1982

Compassion for suffering humanity. The Good News of Jesus Christ brings special meaning to suffering humanity. God's love brings hope to those who live under the bondage of sin, and who are victims of poverty and injustice. We believe that Christians involved in world evangelization should live among people as servants and minister to the needs of the whole person. GREAT COMMISSION MANIFESTO, 1989

3. RACIAL JUSTICE

One race. We recognize the failure of many of us in the recent past to speak with sufficient clarity and force upon the Biblical unity of the human race. All men are one in the humanity created by God Himself. All men are one in their common need of divine redemption, and all are offered salvation in Jesus Christ. All men stand under the same divine condemnation and all must find justification before God in the same way: by faith in Christ, Lord of all and Savior of all who put their trust in Him. All who are "in Christ" henceforth can recognize no distinctions based on race or color and no limitations arising out of human pride or prejudice, whether in the fellowship of those who have come to faith in Christ or in the proclamation of the Good News of Jesus Christ to men everywhere. BERLIN STATEMENT, 1966 (WORLD CONGRESS ON EVANGELISM, BERLIN, 1966)

Human dignity grounded in the image of God. We affirm that God is both the Creator and the Judge of all men and women. We therefore should share his concern for justice and reconciliation throughout human society and for the liberation of men and women from every kind of oppression. Because mankind is made in the image of God, every person, regardless of race, religion, colour, culture, class, gender or age, has an intrinsic dignity because of which he should be respected and served, not exploited. LAUSANNE COVENANT, 1974, PART OF CLAUSE 5

Unity and equality of all. We reject the notion that men are unequal because of distinction of race or color. In the name of Scripture and of Jesus Christ we condemn racialism wherever it appears. We ask forgiveness for our past sins in refusing to recognize the clear command of God to love our fellowmen with a love that transcends every human barrier and prejudice. We seek by God's grace to eradicate from our lives and from our witness whatever is displeasing to Him in our relations one with another. We extend our hands to each other in love, and those same hands reach out to men everywhere with the prayer that the Prince of Peace may soon unite our sorely divided world. BERLIN STATEMENT, 1966 (WORLD CONGRESS ON EVANGELISM, BERLIN, 1966)

Following the way of justice. When our evangelism is linked with concern to alleviate poverty, uphold justice, oppose abuses of secular and economic power, stand against racism, and advance responsible stewardship of the global environment, it reflects the compassion of Christ and may gain an acceptance it would not otherwise receive.

We pledge ourselves to follow the way of justice in our family and social life, and to keep personal, social, and environmental values in view as we evangelize. AMSTERDAM DECLARATION, 2000, CHARTER 11

Resisting all that is incompatible with the kingdom. The proclamation of God's kingdom necessarily demands the prophetic denunciation of all that is incompatible with it. Among the evils we deplore are destructive violence, including institutionalized violence, political corruption, all forms of exploitation of people and of the earth, the undermining of the family, abortion on demand, the drug traffic, and the abuse of human rights. MANILA MANIFESTO, 1989, PART OF CLAUSE A.4

God's call to righteousness. [We believe] that Christians are called to live in daily witness to the grace which comes to us in Jesus Christ, to preach the gospel to every person according to the command of Christ, and to declare God's insistence upon righteousness and justice in all relationships and structures of human society. ASBURY THEOLOGICAL SEMINARY

4. STEWARDSHIP OF CREATION

The ecological crisis. The earth is the Lord's, and the gospel is good news for all creation. Christians share in the responsibility God gave to all humanity to care for the earth. We call on all Christians to commit themselves to ecological integrity in practicing responsible stewardship of creation, and we encourage Christians in environmental care and protection initiatives. IGUASSU AFFIRMATION, 1999, COMMITMENTS 12

Stewardship of God's creation. We are stewards. The resources at our disposal are not our own. They are a sacred trust from God through donors on behalf of the poor. We are faithful to the purpose for which those resources are given and manage them in a manner that brings maximum benefit to the poor. WORLD VISION

Stewards, not proprietors. We are determined, therefore, to honor God as the owner of all things, to remember that we are stewards and not proprietors of any land or property that we may have, to use them in the service of others, and to seek justice with the poor who are exploited and powerless to defend themselves. AN EVANGELICAL COMMITMENT TO SIMPLE LIFE-STYLE, 1980

Call to a simple life. All of us are shocked by the poverty of millions and disturbed by the injustices which cause it. Those of us who live in affluent circumstances accept our duty to develop a simple life-style in order to contribute more generously to both relief and evangelism. (Jn 9:4; Mt 9:35-38; Rom 9:1-3; 1 Cor 9:19-23; Mk 16:15; Is 58:6, 7; Jas 1:27; 2:1-9; Mt 25:31-46; Acts 2:44, 45; 4:34, 35). LAUSANNE COVENANT, 1974, PART OF CLAUSE 9

A just and simple lifestyle. So then, having been freed by the sacrifice of our Lord Jesus Christ, in obedience to his call, in heartfelt compassion for the poor, in concern for evangelism, development and justice, and in solemn anticipation of the Day of Judgement, we humbly commit ourselves to develop a just and simple life-style, to support one another in it and to encourage others to join us in this commitment. AN EVANGELICAL COMMITMENT TO SIMPLE LIFE-STYLE, 1980, OUR RESOLVE

16

THE FUTURE

The Last Things

God's redemptive purpose will be consummated by the return of Christ to raise the dead, to judge all people according to the deeds done in the body and to establish his glorious kingdom. The wicked shall be separated from God's presence, but the righteous in glorious bodies shall live and reign with him forever. Then shall the eager expectation of creation be fulfilled and the whole earth shall proclaim the glory of God who makes all things new.

FULLER THEOLOGICAL SEMINARY:
STATEMENT OF FAITH

1. THE BLESSED HOPE

The blessed hope. We believe in the blessed hope that Jesus Christ will soon return to this earth, personally, visibly, and unexpectedly, in power and great glory, to gather His elect, to raise the dead, to judge the nations, and to bring His Kingdom to fulfillment. WHEATON COLLEGE

His coming again. He shall come again, personally and visibly, to complete His saving work and to consummate the eternal plan of God. GORDON-CONWELL THEOLOGICAL SEMINARY

The fulfillment of his promise. We believe . . . that our Lord Jesus Christ, in fulfillment of His own promise, both angelically and apostolically attested, will personally return in power and great glory. WORLD GOSPEL MISSION

His glorious appearing. We wait for the "blessed hope, the glorious appearing of our great God and Savior, Jesus Christ" (Tit 2:13); and we believe that all things shall finally be subjected to God through Him (1 Cor 15:25-28). HCJB WORLD RADIO/WORLD RADIO MISSIONARY FELLOWSHIP

The consummation of his kingdom. We believe that at a day and hour known only to God, our Lord Jesus Christ shall come again personally, bodily, visibly, gloriously, to consummate His Kingdom of righteousness and peace. TYNDALE UNIVERSITY COLLEGE & SEMINARY

2. PROCLAIMING CHRIST UNTIL HE COMES

Salvation and judgment. We believe that Jesus Christ will return personally and visibly, in power and glory to consummate his salvation and his judgment. This promise of his coming is a further spur to our evangelism, for we remember his words that the gospel must first be preached to all nations. LAUSANNE COVENANT, 1974, PART OF CLAUSE 15

Proclaiming Christ until he comes. We have been told to go to the ends of the earth with the gospel, and we have been promised that the end of the age will come only when we have done so. The two ends (of earth space and time) will coincide. Until then he has pledged to be with us.

So the Christian mission is an urgent task. We do not know how long we have. We certainly have no time to waste. MANILA MANIFESTO, 1989, PART OF CONCLUSION

Though iniquity shall abound. We believe that the later days will be characterized by general lawlessness and departure from the faith; that on the part of the world iniquity shall abound and evil men shall wax worse and worse; that on the part of the Church there will be a falling away and the love of many shall wax cold; that false teachers shall abound, both deceiving and being deceived; and further, that present conditions indicate that we are now living in these perilous times. 1 Tim 4:1, 2; Rom 16:17, 18; 2 Tim 2:1-5, 13; 2 Pet 2:1, 2, 10; Mt 24:11, 12; 2 Thess 2:3. GARDEN CITY CONFESSION OF FAITH, 1998, ARTICLE XIV

3. RESURRECTION AND FINAL JUDGMENT

The resurrection of the just and unjust. [We believe in] the Resurrection of both the saved and the lost; they that are saved unto the resurrection of life, they that are lost unto the resurrection of damnation. WORLD EVANGELICAL ALLIANCE

The resurrection of the body. We believe in the bodily resurrection of the just and unjust, the everlasting punishment of the lost, and the everlasting blessedness of the saved. WHEATON COLLEGE

The final destiny of the righteous and unrighteous. At the end of the age the bodies of the dead shall be raised. The righteous shall enter into full possession of eternal bliss in the presence of God, and the wicked shall be condemned to eternal death. CHRISTIANITY TODAY INTERNATIONAL

Final judgment. We believe in . . . the victorious reign and future personal return of Jesus Christ, who will judge all people with justice and mercy, giving over the unrepentant to eternal condemnation but receiving the redeemed into eternal life. To God be glory forever. INTER-VARSITY CHRISTIAN FELLOWSHIP

4. ETERNAL LIFE

Grace amid death. At death, Christ takes the believer to himself (Phil 1:21) for unimaginable joy in the ceaseless worship of God (Rev 22:1). GOSPEL OF JESUS CHRIST, THE GOSPEL

Heaven. There will be a resurrection of the body for both the saved and unsaved dead (1 Cor 15:16-17, 42-44; Jn 5:29). There will be eternal life and blessedness in heaven for the saved (Jn 14:2-3; Jn 3:16) where they will be in the immediate presence of God (Rev 22:3-4) and will share His eternal reign (Rev 22:5). OMS INTERNATIONAL

Eternal life. All who believe in and receive the Lord Jesus Christ have eternal life; those who do not will be eternally lost (Jn 1:12; Jn 3:36; Rom 10:9; 1 Jn 5:11, 12). HCJB WORLD RADIO/WORLD RADIO MISSIONARY FELLOWSHIP

5. THE LOST

The death of unbelievers. At physical death the unbeliever enters immediately into eternal, conscious separation from the Lord and awaits the resurrection of his body to everlasting judgment and condemnation. CAMPUS CRUSADE FOR CHRIST

Hell. There will be eternal death and punishment for the unsaved in hell, the lake of fire (Rev 20:15) where they shall consciously share the company of the damned (Rev 21:8) in eternal separation from God (2 Thess 1:9), under the punishing wrath of God (Jn 3:26) which will be as eternal for the unsaved as life will be for the saved (Mt 25:46). OMS INTERNATIONAL

6. THE FINAL VICTORY

The end of the age. He will raise the righteous and the unrighteous in their bodies and will judge them to eternal blessing or to eternal punishment. At the end of the age He will make all things new and present the kingdom to God the Father. JAPAN BIBLE SEMINARY

Thy kingdom come. [We believe] in God's ultimate victory over Satan and all evil and the establishment of His perfect kingdom in a new heaven and a new earth. ASBURY THEOLOGICAL SEMINARY

The new heaven and new earth. We believe that Jesus Christ will personally and visibly return in glory to raise the dead and bring salvation and judgment to completion. God will fully manifest His kingdom when He establishes a new heaven and new earth, in which He will be glorified forever and exclude all evil, suffering, and death. PRISON FELLOWSHIP MINISTRIES

The new creation. To those who repent and believe in Christ, God grants a share in the new creation. He gives us new life, which includes the forgiveness of our sins and the indwelling, transforming power of his Spirit. He welcomes us into his new community, which consists of people of all races, nations and cultures. And he promises that one day we will enter his new world, in which evil will be abolished, nature will be redeemed, and God will reign forever.

This good news must be boldly proclaimed, wherever possible, in church and in public halls, on radio and television, and in the open air, because it is God's power for salvation and we are under obligation to make it known. MANILA MANIFESTO, 1989, PART OF CLAUSE A.2

7. DOXOLOGY

Faithfulness to covenant. Therefore, in the light of this our faith and our resolve, we enter into a solemn covenant with God and with each other, to pray, to plan and to work together for the evangelization of the whole world. We call upon others to join us. May God help us by his grace and for his glory to be faithful to this our covenant! Amen, Alleluia! LAUSANNE COVENANT, 1974, CONCLUSION

Intercession. Deliver us from ignorance, error, lovelessness, pride, selfishness, impurity, and cowardice. Enable us to be truthful, kind, humble, sympathetic, pure, and courageous. Salvation belongs to you, O God, who sits on the throne, and to the Lamb. We ask you to make our gospel witness effective. Anoint our proclamation with the Holy Spirit; use it to gather that great multitude from all nations who will one day stand before you and the Lamb giving praise. This we ask by the merits of our Lord Jesus Christ. Amen. AMSTERDAM DECLARATION, 2000, PRAYER

Conclusion

The Evangelical Profile

Our task in this section is to show what may reasonably and fairly be inferred from the array of statements paraded above. But to prepare our readers for assessing the generalizations we will make, we first ask you to stand back with us a little and review the overall profile that empirical evangelicalism presents today worldwide. Here we pick up and expand hints dropped earlier, drawing both on our own knowledge as evangelical insiders and on the many critical analyses—theological, historical, sociological and psychological, technical and popular, friendly and unfriendly—that students of this movement have offered during the past half century.

Theologically, the roots of evangelicalism go back much further than its name, a nineteenth-century coinage, would suggest. Its account of God and godliness builds on the trinitarian, incarnational and transformational consensus that the patristic period achieved, and then on the consensus of the magisterial Reformation about biblical authority and justification by faith only, through grace only, in virtue of Christ only. Within this frame, evangelicalism characteristically emphasizes the penal-substitutionary view of the cross and the radical reality of the Bible-taught, Spirit-wrought inward change, relational and directional, that makes a person a Christian (new birth, regeneration, conversion, faith, repentance, forgiveness, new creation, all in and through Jesus Christ). Building on this foundation, evangelicalism then formulates its consensual view of the universal and local church as a worshiping, witnessing, working fellowship of the faithful, committed to mutual nurture and evangelism and also to neighbor-love as a venture of gentleness that seeks to relieve material and spiritual needs as widely as is possible.

Beyond this point, important differences of style, polity and policy remain among evangelicals who are Lutheran, Reformed, Anglican, Methodist, Baptist and Pentecostal, but the differences are seen as subordinate to these unitive affirmations. Debates still go on between paedobaptists and credo-baptists, liturgical and nonliturgical worshipers, lovers of modern praise songs and devotees of old hymns, classical Calvinists and classical Arminians, cessationists and charismatics, and those who can and cannot endure minority, sore-thumb status in dysfunctional sub-evangelical denominations. But evangelicals' shared view of the Bible and the atonement, of faith and life in Christ, and of the church's nature and mission hold them tightly together, more tightly than used to be the case when denominational walls were higher. As denominations droop and liberal theology grows ever more eccentric, the solidarity developed during the past half century will likely continue.

Many further bonds unite evangelicals, cutting across social spectrums and denominational and national boundaries. Evangelicals see themselves, vocationally, as stewards of God's truth and guardians of his gospel in an age of apostasy; as a renewing and revitalizing force in world Christianity; and as a spearhead of sanity, discipline and reconstruction in a wasteland of antinomian worldliness. They treasure the Bible, the gospel and the ministry of the Holy Spirit as the true secret of personal and corporate spiritual life; confidently they proclaim Christ crucified, risen, reigning and returning as our peace, our path and our prize, even as they humbly beg his mercy for their own salvation. They view the preaching of God's Word as the climax of church worship, the Eucharist being confirmatory of divine grace; they value small Bible study and prayer groups as a key means of maintaining the spiritual life; they believe that spiritual gifts are given to all believers and that every-member ministry in the body of Christ is the cutting-edge principle for congregational advance. It is this combination of distinctives that mark them out from alternative forms of Christian belief and life.

Moreover, a network of seminaries, Bible colleges, institutes, conferences, seminars and personal ministries on radio, TV and tape, as well as a mass of literature from evangelical publishing houses, magazines, media programs and parachurch ministries, plus a flood of Internet material, fertilizes and consolidates the evangelical movement in a way unparalleled elsewhere in the Christian world. Internal activity for enriching the evangelical community knows no bounds. There is also a characteristic evangelical ethos, encouraging and invigorating morale-raising informality in which biblical and theological discussion, personal testimony and extempore prayer are welcomed. Consensus is consolidated against the multiform wasting disease of reductive naturalism and supernaturalized Christianity, along with such social ills as abortion and euthanasia on demand, the weakening of the family, the secularizing of education and the politicized enfranchising of homosexual behavior.

Put all this together and it becomes clear why the evangelical bloc is strong today and why it seems to grow stronger through the prospering of its outreach to younger people. This is the constituency that has produced and that lives by statements of faith such as we have reviewed, a fact we must remember as we reflect on the import of this material.

THE EVANGELICAL CONSENSUS

Our ten concluding observations are as follows:

1. The evangelical consensus focuses on a cohesive account of the canonical Scriptures and their integral canonical interpretation. By canonical Scriptures we mean the sixty-six books of the Protestant Bible, and by canonical interpretation we mean an elucidation that treats this Bible in its entirety as the God-given guide, rule and map for faith and life. Such an elucidation aims to embrace all biblical teaching in a way that observes the inner links between the books themselves and is free from deletion, distortion, incoherence and internal contradiction. This is the kind of interpretation that the universal church has sought constantly to practice in its preaching, teaching, nurturing, catechizing and corrective ministry. So approached and handled, the Bible yields a clear story line, both historical and theological, which the evangelical documents pick up. When, as often, they cite Scripture references, this is not irresponsible proof-texting but a declaration of commitment to engage in exegesis in context. Their statements are offered as a faithful echo of the Bible, proclamatory, practical and with openness to biblical correction should this prove necessary.

2. ***The evangelical consensus sets forth the Christ-centered story of redemption that earlier creeds and confessions also told.*** The documents we have cited present the evangel succinctly as the good news of what the one true God, the triune creator, preserver and providential guide of all history and natural events, has done to save our race from sin, guilt, lostness and final death. Made to bear God's image, all humanity has gone astray and still goes astray. But in Palestine, in Jerusalem, two millennia ago, Jesus Christ the God-man died on a cross to reconcile us to the Father by reconciling the Father to us, as the Father himself had planned. This Jesus is now the risen, reigning Lord, who claims the allegiance of every person everywhere. Salvation, initiated by the Father, is offered through the Son and applied by the Holy Spirit. The Spirit moves us to turn to God in repentance, uniting us with Christ to share his risen life, freeing us from slavery to sin, producing in us his Christlike fruit, and empowering us for service of Christ in the world. Justification and adoption set us right with God relationally, and through regeneration, sanctification and glorification our fallen nature is renewed in Christ's image. All believers in Christ are linked to him and to each other in God's own family, which is the communion of saints. Thus by his word and Spirit the Father through the Son creates and grows his one multinational, multicultural, multigenerational holy catholic and apostolic church, which is called to take the whole gospel to the whole world. For the present, the battle is on in many forms and against many foes as the church tackles this never-ending task in each generation. But it will not always be so; God's redemptive purpose will be consummated by the return of Christ for universal resurrection, universal judgment and universal display of his glorious kingdom, in a

splendor which he and we, his people, the new humanity, will enjoy together for ever.

Because God's general revelation extends everywhere, touches of truth, beauty and goodness will be found in the many non-Christian belief systems, though the only way to know God in peace, love and joy is through Christ. Because all humans are made in God's image, marred in them though it now is, the religious liberty and human rights of all must be defended. As in his own ministry Christ joined works of mercy to his words of grace, so Christians are to add to their verbal witness and pastoral endeavor good works of service to the sick, the hungry, prisoners, the disadvantaged and handicapped, and the oppressed.

Here, in a nutshell, is evangelical faith as embedded and expressed in these consensus-bearing documents. Surely no argument is needed to establish it as wholly in line with the ecumenical creeds, Protestant confessions and mainline theological traditions of earlier times. What we have here, in short, is a version of catholic Christianity, to be acknowledged and assessed as such.

3. The evangelical consensus is internally consistent and comprehensive in its proclamation. When in the English-speaking West in the early twentieth century liberalism gained leadership in what had previously been evangelical denominations, institutions and alliances, adherents of the older paths saw need to identify themselves and their organizations by producing bases of faith of their own. Being occasional and reactionary, with polemical and judgmental undertones, these statements did not always declare essential Christian faith in a well-integrated way. Hence they have created expectations that all evangelical accounts will be eccentric, internally disproportionate and disjointed, and sectarian in tone and tendency, thus lacking long-term theological importance.

At first such thinking was, unfortunately, partially justified. But the array of statements on which we have drawn surely confounds this expectation. The topical sequence and verbal precision of our extracts from them has, we hope, already made this evident. Granted, the number of things evangelicals have to say on a particular topic is to some extent determined by how much has been said against what they are reaffirming, as well as by its intrinsic importance in biblical Christianity as such. In some measure our selections reflect this, as for instance in the space given to elucidations of the supremacy of Scripture. What needs to be grasped, however, is that these latter-day statements are the platform not of defensive huddles and cabals but of interdenominational parachurch mission agencies of many kinds, and they have clearly been so drafted as to constitute in their subtext an invitation—indeed a rallying call—to potential supporters and a unitive reference point for all their actual adherents as they move forward in their defined roles. Of set purpose, therefore, they seek to embody the breadth, wisdom and organic coherence of small-*c* catholic Christianity, the religion that Jesus' apostles set forth as a faith for the world. We think they succeed. The length, breadth, height and depth of authentic biblical Christianity are here, and so is the integrated, organic, Christ-centered, single-ball-of-wax quality of all recorded apostolic thought and teaching. The draftsmanship of these documents fully bears comparison with other forms of words produced in the church during the past half century, and the consensual positions that they state with such coherence, comprehensiveness and clarity are entirely attuned to the New Testament witness.

4. ***The evangelical consensus claims continuity with what faithful Christians have always believed.*** The statements from which our excerpts came were hammered out in dialogue by evangelicals laboring to verbalize the conceptual core not just of their own convictions in their own immediate circumstances but of the faith that all of God's people have held. In other words, whether by deliberate policy or by spontaneous instinct or both, they have sought to show that their assertions match the classic fifth-century rule for recognizing orthodoxy: what has been believed everywhere, always and by all. Distilled by Vincent of Lérins in his *Commonitorium*, this rule, the Vincentian canon as it is commonly called, is in effect a declaration of confidence in the ongoing work of the Holy Spirit teaching God's people God's truth as

set forth in God's Word. This is a ministry of the Spirit that evangelicals, with their strong pneumatology and equally strong distrust of unaided reason and unsanctioned speculation, are very conscious of needing, and on which, constantly and conscientiously, they seek to depend. Thus an attempt to think transgenerationally and transculturally is intrinsic to all evangelical theologizing and all evangelical confessional statements. For whatever their local tactical concerns, evangelicals always aim to bring into focus the true unity and due application (as it is for all periods and cultures) of the once-for-all gospel truth embodied in the holy Scriptures. Truth, unchanged and unchanging in its witness to the Christ who never changes, is what they believe they are dealing with, and they practice conscious loyalty to it and to him who is central to the statements they produce. So the goal of matching the Vincentian requirement has regularly shaped evangelical reflection on what needs to be said here and now in order to safeguard biblical faith amid the cross-currents of our time.

5. The evangelical consensus calls for wholehearted discipleship to our Lord Jesus Christ. People sometimes ask with real puzzlement what makes evangelicals tick, and a stereotype often put forward to answer this question is that they are driven by conservative nostalgia—old-fashioned prejudice in favor of old-time religion and old-time socio-politico-economic conditions. In an era of rapid sociocultural change and of liberal theology constantly reinventing itself in order to keep up with the wider world, the welcome given to this stereotype is understandable, the more so since evangelicals whom the cap fits undoubtedly exist.

But across the board, and certainly in the many circles where the evangelical future is discussed, this stereotype proves totally false. Comfort-zone conservatism, unexamined and uncritiqued, is not the name of the evangelical game, and our documents show this. They make it clear that the evangelical way, as a matter of conscience, is to judge both present and past by the light of Scripture and, in behavior as well as in belief, to retain only that which, when the heritage is thus sifted, appears good, right and relevant by biblical standards. Evangelicals, one might say, are critical conservationists rather than knee-jerk conservative reactionaries. Moreover, the documents show evangelicals accepting social accountability and resolving on action in such matters as care for the poor, environmental stewardship and human rights. Evangelical motives are not politicized—Archie Bunker is not an evangelical role model, and Samaritan's Purse is not a power game in disguise. Instead evangelicals call each other to selfless service in unrewarding situations in order to make bad things less bad and to set good things going. Why? What drives them? Not gain, not glory and clearly not a passion for things past. What, then? The question presses.

In fact, the answer is very clear if one reads between the lines of our excerpts. These consensual statements are human products, and human heartbeats can be heard within them, at least by those who have ears for such things. The statements are not only doctrinal testimonies defining discipleship against delusions of one sort or another. They are also devotional utterances pointing to the imperatives of love for God and neighbor and drawing their force from the following realization: Jesus Christ, the man of Galilee, the incarnate Son of God, is real and alive today, and Christians who live through him must ever live to him, with a personal loyalty and commitment corresponding to that of those who literally followed him round Palestine in the days of his flesh.

Evangelicals know firsthand three truths that are indelibly inscribed on every regenerate heart: we are to honor, glorify and serve God because he is God (the creational insight that is basic to God's claim on us); we are to express gratitude in response to the goodness and grace shown to us (the redemptive insight into the immeasurable debt of love that we owe to the holy Three); and we are to do good to others (the societal insight into the form of community life that is fitting and fulfilling for all humans as God has designed us, which is also a matter of Christ's command to all Christians as his followers and disciples). Believers, who are new creatures in Christ, find that their instinct and supreme wish, as well as their calling and supreme task, is to live out all three insights together. The three in combination thus become the motivating force that drives evangelicals in their many endeavors. No longer slaves of sin, they serve righteousness, seeking to please their Lord in everything. But this is a state of mind and heart that only believers know; the world has never understood it and can never understand it. It is the way of life in the Lord.

6. The evangelical consensus understands the church to be continually in mission as an expression of discipleship to Jesus Christ. The spreading of the gospel (mission, as it is called these days, accenting Christians' part in it) has always been a major evangelical concern. The church has been well described as a society existing for the benefit of those outside it, and this viewpoint is reflected in the missional commitment that these statements spell out. It may fairly be said that Protestant liberalism has given up on crosscultural church-planting action; Eastern Orthodoxy practices a measure of what may be called in-drag and inflow but with few exceptions can hardly be labeled outreach; Roman Catholicism struggles with the implications of the new evangelization for which John Paul II has called; and in terms of hands-on evangelistic action worldwide, evangelicalism has led the field throughout the fifty-year span of this study. The statements from Lausanne, Manila and Amsterdam in particular reinforce and resource global evangelism; that is what they were for. They should be seen as a series of attempts to spell out the Great Commission of Matthew 28:19-20, the church's marching orders from Christ its Head. In that sense they are not so much guides to pedantic theology as a call to apostolic passion in the action of taking the word of Christ to the world. Evangelicals must not lose sight of their belief that faithful discipleship requires prayerful and practical commitment to this enterprise, for it is integral to the consensus that we are examining.

7. The evangelical consensus has extended its doctrinal range. Part of the story our documents tell is that during the past half century, evangelicals, striving side by side to maintain biblical orthodoxy, have discovered a deeper and wider measure of unity in this truth than they previously knew they had. After bringing separate evangelical groups together for practical cooperation in mission, God is now unifying previously separated—one might even say balkanized—streams of evangelical theological witness. For evangelicals have been discovering a united mind on matters about which they thought themselves divided—as, indeed, older generations of theological polemicists and newer brands of theological irenicists had told them they were. This has happened strikingly in both the basic fields of the Reformation conflict, the doctrine of the nature and authority of Scripture, and the doctrine of the meaning and grounds of justification by faith, matters on which a number of loose ends had been hanging out.

With regard to Scripture, the International Council on Biblical Inerrancy (ICBI) was formed at a time when the idea of biblical infallibility without inerrancy had made some headway. Between 1978 and 1988, however, ICBI produced a series of carefully crafted books and statements on which most evangelicals converged, so laying the reduced and vulnerable view of the authority of Scripture to rest and finding a doctrinal solidarity that had not previously seemed to be there. With regard to justification, disagreements on details had caused flutterings in evangelical dovecotes ever since the days of Wesley, but the consensus statement *The Gospel of Jesus Christ: An Evangelical Celebration*, published in 1999, was endorsed by several hundred leaders from all evangelical traditions. The statement spelled out more fully and precisely the imputed righteousness of Christ as the ground for our pardon and acceptance than any representative evangelical statement had yet done. Once more, a doctrinal solidarity appeared that hitherto had not seemed to be there, and once more dubious-sounding views were laid to rest.

Our extended quotations from the key documents in both cases have already laid out the consensus that now exists. The increased evangelical concern for and achievement of clarity in communal confession on major matters bodes well for the future of the movement, not simply as an ad hoc pragmatist-pietist alliance but as a responsible ongoing witness to the essential, unchanging truth of God.

8. ***The evangelical consensus shows a deepening concern for Christian unity in profession, proclamation and pastoral care.*** As the new

millennium opens, evangelicals are present and active within widely varying denominational structures, liturgical patterns and styles, historical identities, congregations of varied shapes and sizes, types of polity and pathways of discipline, both within and outside what is nowadays called the mainline church. Many non-Protestants, including Catholics and Orthodox, are finding it possible to join in action with heirs of the magisterial Reformation. The evangelical consensus is being affirmed more widely in the historic peace churches, the remnants of Protestant separatism, and especially in younger Christian bodies in the Two-Thirds world that seek mutual ministry and encouragement.

Formerly, parachurch evangelical movements, organized as societies or alliances for accomplishing specific objectives, were thought of as merely auxiliary to the denominations and thus of secondary importance. Now, however, with denominations receding in significance and themselves becoming secondary realities on the world Christian stage, evangelicalism is insisting more forthrightly that its transdenominational, transconfessional, transcultural unity of Bible-based faith points the way for the church of tomorrow. Anglican, Lutheran, Reformed, Baptist, Congregational, Wesleyan, Pentecostal, revivalist, separatist, holiness, charismatic and many more streams of testimony to the gospel flow together into the evangelical confession. As liberal churches become more anti-confessional, evangelicalism grows more intentionally confessional in spirit, with an increasing concern to display evangelical practice as a living out of Christ's basic requirements according to the New Testament. As the older Protestant churches become in this regard less churchly, evangelicalism, with its vivid transdenominational sense of Christian identity, steps forward to take up the slack.

Not that evangelicals are anti-denominational, as is sometimes thought. They are, in fact, more at home, so far as faith goes, within the older denominational traditions than are those who frantically try to tailor their faith to modern consciousness or catch up with the latest in cultural fads. But evangelicals are characteristically attuned to local congregations rather than to denominations as such, and they ordinarily act on the principle that God does not ask his servants to settle for life in, as it were, an empty refrigerator, where the warm teaching and fellowship needed to nurture them and theirs is missing. The result is that during the course of their life they may well change congregations across denominational lines. Their constant concern is that the Bible and its gospel should be faithfully ministered in their place of worship, and their allegiance usually goes to church communities where this is actually happening.

9. ***The evangelical consensus is an ecumenically significant reality.*** The confessional utterances on which we have drawn all follow the expository sequence of the great ecumenical creeds, the Apostles' and the Nicene, an order that is also followed by (for instance) Peter Lombard's *Sentences*, Melanchthon's *Loci*, Calvin's *Institutes*, John Pearson on the Apostles' Creed and many later systematic surveys of the faith. This consistency of sequence is no accident; it reflects the insight that the Trinity is the basic biblical frame for embracing the whole of Christian truth and that the Christian message comes clearest to the mind when set out in three substantive sections: creation and providence as the work of the Father, the architect of everything; reconciliation and resurrection, redemption, restoration and reward as the gracious work of the Son, the mediator of everything; and forgiveness with fellowship, church with sacrament, and new life with new hope as the gracious work of the Holy Spirit, the handcrafter and finisher of everything. While all three divine persons are personally involved in all divine works, and while no one of them does or, it seems, could act alone, the Bible usually gives primacy of focus to one over the other two when dealing with the three discernible areas of divine activity of which we have just spoken. So the Father is revealed as creating, the Son as redeeming and the Spirit as renewing. The historic creeds follow the Bible in this, and so today do evangelical declarations. As a bulwark against the implicit unitarianism that is endemic to liberal theology, this traditional way of stating things has value for the worldwide church in every age. It cannot be bettered, and no alternative arrangement of the material is so good. The evangelical consensus thus serves the church well by adhering to the old path at this point.

10. ***The evangelical consensus is evidently here to stay.*** The consensus documented in these pages stems from half a century of convergence among independent parachurch associations and institutions, all of them to a greater or lesser extent missional, educational, remedial and (to use the old word) charitable in purpose. They were also born of a sense that the churches were not doing enough—in many cases, not doing anything—of what needed to be done in areas where Christian action was called for. Sometimes polemically, more often irenically, these organizations affirmed evangelical faith with avowedly doxological intent, seeking to honor God by spreading gospel truth and supporting gospel ministries of all kinds.

The world-embracing zeal of missionary pioneers, the passionate biblical focus of Bible teachers and Bible conference organizers, outrage at the way liberal leaders misled the churches and misconceived Christian mission, plus bold dreams of one day beating liberals at their own academic and sociocultural game all contributed to the development of this family of parachurch groups, and gave it, under God, a virility and toughness that overcame many discouragements and achieved remarkable gains on many fronts. Its reformational convictions, pietistic priorities, resources of money and literature, and aggressive pastoral strategies and programs, all driven by evangelistic passion and commitment to work hard for God, have made it a force to be reckoned with. Attacks on its integrity (basically two: that it is intellectually obscurantist and unsustainable and that it is too much the plaything of its own strong leaders) have been answered convincingly. It has become as mature in its style, as accountable to its supporters and as transparent to those outside of it as such a movement (a veritable anthill of independent units) can well be. All the signs point to it continuing indefinitely as what it is today.

As the liberal-led denominational churches languish, so the evangelical sense of churchly responsibility—responsibility, that is, to plant, tend, service and support new congregations and to help revive others that are dying—seems to grow. Maybe it was not always so, but it is so now, and this too seems likely to continue. The evangelicalism of the present consensus is not sectarian and separatist but pastoral, unitive and convergent, and all who care about Christianity's future need to be abreast of it. It is here to stay. The older ecumenical movement, now evidently running out of steam, was once called the great new fact of our time; it seems clear that the developed, and developing, evangelical movement has a much better claim to be so described.

We have documented evangelicals' consensual faith not only for straight-through reading but for future reference as needed. We now invite Orthodox, Roman Catholic, liberal and secular inquirers and critics to examine the exegetical ground, biblical faithfulness, theological viability, rational plausibility and ecumenical potential of this belief-system. It is the creed of a very large and still growing bloc of the world's believers, it boldly claims the high ground of biblical centrism, and it ought to be taken account of.

The Evangelical Resurgence

We have tried to avoid advocacy and confine ourselves to factual comments that may help in understanding the material. As we close, however, we must briefly show our hand and state our hope for the constituency whose consensus we have distilled above.

We see evangelicalism as essentially a Spirit-led movement for recovery and renewal. The recovery is of catholic biblical truth, classic Christian wisdom, piercing proclamation of Jesus Christ as Lord and Savior, knowledge of sin requiring repentance, and energy in the Spirit for worship, witness and service. Announcing, inducing and expressing new life in Christ has always been the church's prime task, but there are periods of time—such as ours—when the church slips and to some extent loses touch with its task. When this happens, the phenomenon called evangelicalism is, in essence, a movement of the Holy Spirit to recall the church to its roots and awaken it to its proper business. Thus evangelicalism is first a God-given stewardship of gospel truth and then a God-sent force for reviving, revitalizing and reforming what has become deformed in personal faith and spirituality, pastoral nurture and discipline, theological witness and education, and evangelistic outreach to a lost world. Evangelicalism is a restoring of ideals of doctrinal purity, Christlike character and conduct, good personal spiritual health, worship with eagerness and joyful passion, and church growth according to the Scriptures, that is, qualitative first (see Eph 4:11-16) and quantitative within that frame. (Many evangelicals fault the church-growth movement for putting numbers before quality.) The evangelical consensus guards the evangelical reality, which is essentially new life coming into, and going out from, the community of God's people, according to God's own Word.

Evangelicalism is poised to be blessed by God as the wave of the future because of the truth and life that it brings. Today's church and today's world need both. The movement's own sense of churchly identity and responsibility seem to be on the increase; if so, this is the Spirit of God matching evangelicalism to the deepest needs of our time.

We recognize that evangelicalism may not become the wave of the future, both because of inner weaknesses that may develop and also because the liberalism that rode so high in Protestant churches a century ago still thinks of the movement as poison and can be expected to block it to its own dying day (which yet may not be too far off). But we hope most sincerely that evangelicalism will be the wave of the future, because the renewing of the church does not seem possible without it and because fresh spiritual, moral, intellectual and doxological power in the church is what most of all we long to see.

The Anglican Prayer Book Collect for the fourth Sunday in Advent, for all its archaic idiom, at this point speaks our heart:

> O Lord, raise up (we pray thee) thy power, and come among us, and with great might succour us; that whereas, through our sins and wickedness, we are sore let and hindered in running the race that is set before us, thy bountiful grace and mercy may speedily help and deliver us; through the satisfaction of thy Son our Lord, to whom with thee and the Holy Ghost be honour and glory, world without end. *Amen.*

Appendix A

Lausanne Covenant, 1974

Introduction

We, members of the Church of Jesus Christ, from more than 150 nations, participants in the International Congress On World Evangelization at Lausanne, praise God for his great salvation and rejoice in the fellowship he has given us with himself and with each other. We are deeply stirred by what God is doing in our day, moved to penitence by our failures and challenged by the unfinished task of evangelization. We believe the gospel is God's good news for the whole world, and we are determined by his grace to obey Christ's commission to proclaim it to all mankind and to make disciples of every nation. We desire, therefore, to affirm our faith and our resolve, and to make public our covenant.

1. The Purpose of God

We affirm our belief in the one eternal God, Creator and Lord of the world, Father, Son and Holy Spirit, who governs all things according to the purpose of his will. He has been calling out from the world a people for himself, and sending his people back into the world to be his servants and his witnesses, for the extension of his kingdom, the building up of Christ's body, and the glory of his name. We confess with shame that we have often denied our calling and failed in our mission, by becoming conformed to the world or by withdrawing from it. Yet we rejoice that even when borne by earthen vessels the gospel is still a precious treasure. To the task of making that treasure known in the power of the Holy Spirit we desire to dedicate ourselves anew.
(Is 40:28; Mt 28:19; Eph 1:11; Acts 15:14; Jn 17:6, 18; Eph 4:12; 1 Cor 5:10; Rom 12:2; 2 Cor 4:7)

2. The Authority and Power of the Bible

We affirm the divine inspiration, truthfulness and authority of both Old and New Testament Scriptures in their entirety as the only written Word of God, without error in all that it affirms, and the only infallible rule of faith and practice. We also affirm the power of God's Word to accomplish his purpose of salvation. The message of the Bible is addressed to all men and women. God's revelation in Christ and in Scripture is unchangeable and through it the Holy Spirit still speaks today. He illumines the minds of God's people in every culture to perceive its truth freshly through their own eyes and thus discloses to the whole church ever more of the many-coloured wisdom of God.
(2 Tim 3:16; 2 Pet 1:21; Jn 10:35; Is 55:11; 1 Cor 1:21; Rom 1:16; Mt 5:17, 18; Jude 3; Eph 1:17, 18; 3:10, 18)

3. The Uniqueness and Universality of Christ

We affirm that there is only one Saviour and only one gospel, although there is a wide diversity of evangelistic approaches. We recognize that all men and women have some knowledge of God through his general revelation in nature. But we deny that this can save, for men and women suppress the truth by their unrighteousness. We also reject as derogatory to Christ and the gospel every kind of syncretism and dialogue which implies that Christ speaks equally through all religions and ideologies. Jesus Christ, being himself the only God-man, who gave himself as the only ransom for sinners, is the only mediator between God and man. There is no other name by which we must be saved. All men and women are perishing because of sin, but God loves all men and women, not wishing that any should perish but that all should repent. Yet those who reject Christ repudiate the joy of salvation and condemn themselves to eternal separation from God. To proclaim Jesus as "the Saviour of the world" is not to affirm that all men and women are either automatically or ultimately saved, still less to affirm that all religions offer salvation in Christ. Rather it is to proclaim God's love for a world of sinners and to invite all men and women to respond to him as Saviour and Lord in the wholehearted per-

sonal commitment of repentance and faith. Jesus Christ has been exalted above every other name; we long for the day when every knee shall bow to him and every tongue shall confess him Lord.
(Gal 1:6-9; Rom 1:18-32; 1 Tim 2:5, 6; Acts 4:12; Jn 3:16-19; 2 Pet 3:9; 2 Thess 1:7-9; Jn 4:42; Mt 11:28; Eph 1:20, 21; Phil 2:9-11)

4. The Nature of Evangelism

To evangelize is to spread the good news that Jesus Christ died for our sins and was raised from the dead according to the Scriptures, and that as the reigning Lord he now offers the forgiveness of sins and the liberating gift of the Spirit to all who repent and believe. Our Christian presence in the world is indispensable to evangelism, and so is that kind of dialogue whose purpose is to listen sensitively in order to understand. But evangelism itself is the proclamation of the historical, biblical Christ as Saviour and Lord, with a view to persuading people to come to him personally and so be reconciled to God. In issuing the gospel invitation we have no liberty to conceal the cost of discipleship. Jesus still calls all who would follow him to deny themselves, take up their cross, and identify themselves with his new community. The results of evangelism include obedience to Christ, incorporation into his church and responsible service in the world.
(1 Cor 15:3, 4; Acts 2:32-39; Jn 20:21; 1 Cor 1:23; 2 Cor 4:5; 5:11, 20; Lk 14:25-33; Mk 8:34; Acts 2:40, 47; Mk 10:43-45)

5. Christian Social Responsibility

We affirm that God is both the Creator and the Judge of all men and women. We therefore should share his concern for justice and reconciliation throughout human society and for the liberation of men and women from every kind of oppression. Because mankind is made in the image of God, every person, regardless of race, religion, colour, culture, class, gender or age, has an intrinsic dignity because of which he should be respected and served, not exploited. Here too we express penitence both for our neglect and for having sometimes regarded evangelism and

social concern as mutually exclusive. Although reconciliation with man is not reconciliation with God, nor is social action evangelism, nor is political liberation salvation, nevertheless we affirm that evangelism and socio-political involvement are both part of our Christian duty. For both are necessary expressions of our doctrines of God and man, our love for our neighbour and our obedience to Jesus Christ. The message of salvation implies also a message of judgment upon every form of alienation, oppression and discrimination, and we should not be afraid to denounce evil and injustice wherever they exist. When people receive Christ they are born again into his kingdom and must seek not only to exhibit but also to spread its righteousness in the midst of an unrighteous world. The salvation we claim should be transforming us in the totality of our personal and social responsibilities. Faith without works is dead.
(Acts 17:26, 31; Gen 18:25; Is 1:17; Ps 45:7; Gen 1:26, 27; Jas 3:9; Lev 19:18; Lk 6:27, 35; Jas 2:14-26; Jn 3:3, 5; Mt 5:20; 6:33; 2 Cor 3:18; Jas 2:20)

6. THE CHURCH AND EVANGELISM

We affirm that Christ sends his redeemed people into the world as the Father sent him, and that this calls for a similar deep and costly penetration of the world. We need to break out of our ecclesiastical ghettos and permeate non-Christian society. In the church's mission of sacrificial service evangelism is primary. World evangelization requires the whole church to take the whole gospel to the whole world. The church is at the very centre of God's cosmic purpose and is his appointed means of spreading the gospel. But a church which preaches the cross must itself be marked by the cross. It becomes a stumbling block to evangelism when it betrays the gospel or lacks a living faith in God, a genuine love for people, or scrupulous honesty in all things including promotion and finance. The church is the community of God's people rather than an institution, and must not be identified with any particular culture, social or political system, or human ideology.
(Jn 17:18; 20:21; Mt 28:19, 20; Acts 1:8; 20:27; Eph 1:9, 10; 3:9-11; Gal 6:14, 17; 2 Cor 6:3, 4; 2 Tim 2:19-21; Phil 1:27)

7. Cooperation in Evangelism

We affirm that the church's visible unity in truth is God's purpose. Evangelism also summons us to unity, because our oneness strengthens our witness, just as our disunity undermines our gospel of reconciliation. We recognize, however, that organizational unity may take many forms and does not necessarily forward evangelism. Yet we who share the same biblical faith should be closely united in fellowship, work and witness. We confess that our testimony has sometimes been marred by sinful individualism and needless duplication. We pledge ourselves to seek a deeper unity in truth, worship, holiness and mission. We urge the development of regional and functional cooperation for the furtherance of the church's mission, for strategic planning, for mutual encouragement, and for the sharing of resources, and experience.
(Jn 17:21, 23; Eph 4:3, 4; Jn 13:35; Phil 1:27; Jn 17:11-23)

8. Churches in Evangelistic Partnership

We rejoice that a new missionary era has dawned. The dominant role of western missions is fast disappearing. God is raising up from the younger churches a great new resource for world evangelization, and is thus demonstrating that the responsibility to evangelize belongs to the whole body of Christ. All churches should therefore be asking God and themselves what they should be doing both to reach their own area and to send missionaries to other parts of the world. A re-evaluation of our missionary responsibility and role should be continuous. Thus a growing partnership of churches will develop and the universal character of Christ's church will be more clearly exhibited. We also thank God for agencies which labour in Bible translation, theological education, the mass media, Christian literature, evangelism, missions, church renewal and other specialist fields. They too should engage in constant self-examination to evaluate their effectiveness as part of the Church's mission.
(Rom 1:8; Phil 1:5; 4:15; Acts 13:1-3; 1 Thess 1:6-8)

9. The Urgency of the Evangelistic Task

More than 2,700 million people, which is more than two-thirds of mankind, have yet to be evangelized. We are ashamed that so many have been neglected; it is a standing rebuke to us and to the whole church. There is now, however, in many parts of the world an unprecedented receptivity to the Lord Jesus Christ. We are convinced that this is the time for churches and para-church agencies to pray earnestly for the salvation of the unreached and to launch new efforts to achieve world evangelization. A reduction of foreign missionaries and money in an evangelized country may sometimes be necessary to facilitate the national church's growth in self-reliance and to release resources for unevangelized areas. Missionaries should flow ever more freely from and to all six continents in a spirit of humble service. The goal should be, by all available means and at the earliest possible time, that every person will have the opportunity to hear, understand, and receive the good news. We cannot hope to attain this goal without sacrifice. All of us are shocked by the poverty of millions and disturbed by the injustices which cause it. Those of us who live in affluent circumstances accept our duty to develop a simple life-style in order to contribute more generously to both relief and evangelism.
(Jn 9:4; Mt 9:35-38; Rom 9:1-3; 1 Cor 9:19-23; Mk 16:15; Is 58:6, 7; Jas 1:27; 2:1-9; Mt 25:31-46; Acts 2:44, 45; 4:34, 35)

10. Evangelism and Culture

The development of strategies for world evangelization calls for imaginative pioneering methods. Under God, the result will be the rise of churches deeply rooted in Christ and closely related to their culture. Culture must always be tested and judged by Scripture. Because man is God's creature, some of his culture is rich in beauty and goodness. Because he has fallen, all of it is tainted with sin and some of it is demonic. The gospel does not presuppose the superiority of any culture to another, but evaluates all cultures according to its own criteria of truth and righteousness, and insists on moral absolutes in every culture. Missions

have all too frequently exported with the gospel an alien culture, and churches have sometimes been in bondage to culture rather than to the Scripture. Christ's evangelists must humbly seek to empty themselves of all but their personal authenticity in order to become the servants of others, and churches must seek to transform and enrich culture, all for the glory of God.
(Mk 7:8, 9, 13; Gen 4:21, 22; 1 Cor 9:19-23; Phil 2:5-7; 2 Cor 4:5)

11. Education and Leadership

We confess that we have sometimes pursued church growth at the expense of church depth, and divorced evangelism from Christian nurture. We also acknowledge that some of our missions have been too slow to equip and encourage national leaders to assume their rightful responsibilities. Yet we are committed to indigenous principles, and long that every church will have national leaders who manifest a Christian style of leadership in terms not of domination but of service. We recognize that there is a great need to improve theological education, especially for church leaders. In every nation and culture there should be an effective training programme for pastors and laymen in doctrine, discipleship, evangelism, nurture and service. Such training programmes should not rely on any stereotyped methodology but should be developed by creative local initiatives according to biblical standards.
(Col 1:27, 28; Acts 14:23; Tit 1:5, 9; Mk 10:42-45; Eph 4:11, 12)

12. Spiritual Conflict

We believe that we are engaged in constant spiritual warfare with the principalities and powers of evil, who are seeking to overthrow the church and frustrate its task of world evangelization. We know our need to equip ourselves with God's armour and to fight this battle with the spiritual weapons of truth and prayer. For we detect the activity of our enemy, not only in false ideologies outside the church, but also inside it in false gospels which twist Scripture and put man in the place of

God. We need both watchfulness and discernment to safeguard the biblical gospel. We acknowledge that we ourselves are not immune to worldliness of thought and action, that is, to a surrender to secularism. For example, although careful studies of church growth, both numerical and spiritual, are right and valuable, we have sometimes neglected them. At other times, desirous to ensure a response to the gospel, we have compromised our message, manipulated our hearers through pressure techniques, and become unduly preoccupied with statistics or even dishonest in our use of them. All this is worldly. The church must be in the world; the world must not be in the church.
(Eph 6:12; 2 Cor 4:3, 4; Eph 6:11, 13-18; 2 Cor 10:3-5; 1 Jn 2:18-26; 4:1-3; Gal 1:6-9; 2 Cor 2:17; 4:2; Jn 17:15)

13. Freedom and Persecution

It is the God-appointed duty of every government to secure conditions of peace, justice and liberty in which the church may obey God, serve the Lord Christ, and preach the gospel without interference. We therefore pray for the leaders of the nations and call upon them to guarantee freedom of thought and conscience, and freedom to practise and propagate religion in accordance with the will of God and as set forth in The Universal Declaration of Human Rights. We also express our deep concern for all who have been unjustly imprisoned, and especially for our brethren who are suffering for their testimony to the Lord Jesus. We promise to pray and work for their freedom. At the same time we refuse to be intimidated by their fate. God helping us, we too will seek to stand against injustice and to remain faithful to the gospel, whatever the cost. We do not forget the warnings of Jesus that persecution is inevitable.
(1 Tim 1:1-4; Acts 4:19; 5:29; Col 3:24; Heb 13:1-3; Lk 4:18; Gal 5:11; 6:12; Mt 5:10-12; Jn 15:18-21)

14. The Power of the Holy Spirit

We believe in the power of the Holy Spirit. The Father sent his Spirit to bear witness to his Son; without his witness ours is futile. Conviction of

sin, faith in Christ, new birth and Christian growth are all his work. Further, the Holy Spirit is a missionary spirit; thus evangelism should arise spontaneously from a spirit-filled church. A church that is not a missionary church is contradicting itself and quenching the Spirit. Worldwide evangelization will become a realistic possibility only when the Spirit renews the church in truth and wisdom, faith, holiness, love and power. We therefore call upon all Christians to pray for such a visitation of the sovereign Spirit of God that all his fruit may appear in all his people and that all his gifts may enrich the body of Christ. Only then will the whole church become a fit instrument in his hands, that the whole earth may hear his voice.
(1 Cor 2:4; Jn 15:26, 27; 16:8-11; 1 Cor 12:3; Jn 3:6-8; 2 Cor 3:18; Jn 7:37-39; 1 Thess 5:19; Acts 1:8; Ps 85:4-7; 67:1-3; Gal 5:22, 23; 1 Cor 12:4-31; Rom 12:3-8)

15. The Return of Christ

We believe that Jesus Christ will return personally and visibly, in power and glory to consummate his salvation and his judgment. This promise of his coming is a further spur to our evangelism, for we remember his words that the gospel must first be preached to all nations. We believe that the interim period between Christ's ascension and return is to be filled with the mission of the people of God, who have no liberty to stop before the End. We also remember his warning that false Christs and false prophets will arise as precursors of the final Antichrist. We therefore reject as a proud, self-confident dream the notion that man can ever build a utopia on earth. Our Christian confidence is that God will perfect his kingdom, and we look forward with eager anticipation to that day, and to the new heaven and earth in which righteousness will dwell and God will reign for ever. Meanwhile, we rededicate ourselves to the service of Christ and of men and women in joyful submission to his authority over the whole of our lives.
(Mk 14:62; Heb 9:28; Mk 13:10; Acts 1:8-11; Mt 28:20; Mk 13:21-23; Jn 2:18; 4:1-3; Lk 12:32; Rev 21:1-5; 2 Pet 3:13; Mt 28:18)

CONCLUSION

Therefore, in the light of this our faith and our resolve, we enter into a solemn covenant with God and with each other, to pray, to plan and to work together for the evangelization of the whole world. We call upon others to join us. May God help us by his grace and for his glory to be faithful to this our covenant! Amen, Alleluia!

Appendix B

The Gospel of Jesus Christ

An Evangelical Celebration
1999

For God so loved the world
that he gave his one and only Son,
that whoever believes in him
shall not perish
but have eternal life.

JOHN 3:16

Sing to the LORD, *for he has done glorious things;*
let this be known to all the world.

ISAIAH 12:5

Preamble

The Gospel of Jesus Christ is news, good news: the best and most important news that any human being ever hears.

This Gospel declares the only way to know God in peace, love, and joy is through the reconciling death of Jesus Christ the risen Lord.

This Gospel is the central message of the Holy Scriptures, and is the true key to understanding them.

This Gospel identifies Jesus Christ, the Messiah of Israel, as the Son of God and God the Son, the second Person of the Holy Trinity, whose incarnation, ministry, death, resurrection, and ascension fulfilled the Father's saving will. His death for sins and his resurrection from the dead were promised beforehand by the prophets and attested by eyewitnesses. In God's own time and in God's own way, Jesus Christ shall return as glorious Lord and Judge of all (1 Thess 4:13-18; Mt 25:31-32). He is now giving the Holy Spirit from the Father to all those who are truly his. The three Persons of the Trinity thus combine in the work of saving sinners.

This Gospel sets forth Jesus Christ as the living Savior, Master, Life, and Hope of all who put their trust in him. It tells us that the eternal destiny of all people depends on whether they are savingly related to Jesus Christ.

This Gospel is the only Gospel: there is no other; and to change its substance is to pervert and indeed destroy it. This Gospel is so simple that small children can understand it, and it is so profound that studies by the wisest theologians will never exhaust its riches.

All Christians are called to unity in love and unity in truth. As evangelicals who derive our very name from the Gospel, we celebrate this great good news of God's saving work in Jesus Christ as the true bond of Christian unity, whether among organized churches and denominations or in the many transdenominational cooperative enterprises of Christians together.

The Bible declares that all who truly trust in Christ and his Gospel are sons and daughters of God through grace, and hence are our brothers and sisters in Christ.

All who are justified experience reconciliation with the Father, full remission of sins, transition from the kingdom of darkness to the kingdom of light, the reality of being a new creature in Christ, and the fellowship of the Holy Spirit. They enjoy access to the Father with all the peace and joy that this brings.

The Gospel requires of all believers worship, which means constant praise and giving of thanks to God, submission to all that he has revealed in his written Word, prayerful dependence on him, and vigilance lest his truth be even inadvertently compromised or obscured.

To share the joy and hope of this Gospel is a supreme privilege. It is also an abiding obligation, for the Great Commission of Jesus Christ still stands: proclaim the Gospel everywhere, he said, teaching, baptizing, and making disciples.

By embracing the following declaration we affirm our commitment to this task, and with it our allegiance to Christ himself, to the Gospel itself, and to each other as fellow evangelical believers.

The Gospel

This Gospel of Jesus Christ which God sets forth in the infallible Scriptures combines Jesus' own declaration of the present reality of the kingdom of God with the apostles' account of the person, place, and work of Christ, and how sinful humans benefit from it. The Patristic Rule of Faith, the historic creeds, the Reformation confessions, and the doctrinal bases of later evangelical bodies all witness to the substance of this biblical message.

The heart of the Gospel is that our holy, loving Creator, confronted with human hostility and rebellion, has chosen in his own freedom and faithfulness to become our holy, loving Redeemer and Restorer. The Father has sent the Son to be the Savior of the world (1 Jn 4:14): it is through his one and only Son that God's one and only plan of salvation is implemented. So Peter announced: "Salvation is found in no one else, for there is no other name under heaven given to men by which we must be saved" (Acts 4:12). And Christ himself taught: "I am the way, the truth and the life. No one comes to the Father except through me" (Jn 14:6).

Man. Through the Gospel we learn that we human beings, who were made for fellowship with God, are by nature—that is, "in Adam" (1 Cor 15:22)—dead in sin, unresponsive to and separated from our Maker. We are constantly twisting his truth, breaking his law, belittling his goals and standards, and offending his holiness by our unholiness, so that we truly are "without hope and without God in the world" (Rom 1:18-32; 3:9-20; Eph 2:1-3, 12). Yet God in grace took the initiative to reconcile us to himself through the sinless life and vicarious death of his beloved Son (Eph 2:4-10; Rom 3:21-24).

Atonement. The Father sent the Son to free us from the dominion of sin and Satan, and to make us God's children and friends. Jesus paid our penalty in our place on his cross, satisfying the retributive demands of divine justice by shedding his blood in sacrifice and so making possible justification for all who trust in him (Rom 3:25-26). The Bible describes this mighty substitutionary transaction as the achieving of ransom, reconciliation, redemption, propitiation, and conquest of evil powers (Mt 20:28; 2 Cor 5:18-21; Rom 3:23-25; Jn 12:31; Col 2:15). It secures for us a restored relationship with God that brings pardon and peace, acceptance and access, and adoption into God's family (Col 1:20; 2:13-14; Rom 5:1-2; Gal 4:4-7; 1 Pet 3:18). The faith in God and in Christ to which the Gospel calls us is a trustful outgoing of our hearts to lay hold of these promised and proffered benefits.

This Gospel further proclaims the bodily resurrection, ascension, and enthronement of Jesus as evidence of the efficacy of his once-for-all sacrifice for us, of the reality of his present personal ministry to us, and of the certainty of his future return to glorify us (1 Cor 15; Heb 1:1-4; 2:1-18; 4:14-16; 7:1—10:25). In the life of faith as the Gospel presents it, believers are united with their risen Lord, communing with him, and looking to him in repentance and hope for empowering through the Holy Spirit, so that henceforth they may not sin but serve him truly.

Justification. God's justification of those who trust him, according to the Gospel, is a decisive transition, here and now, from a state of condemnation and wrath because of their sins to one of acceptance and favor by virtue of Jesus' flawless obedience culminating in his voluntary sin-bearing death. God "justifies the wicked" (ungodly: Rom 4:5) by imputing (reckoning, crediting, counting, accounting) righteousness to them and ceasing to count their sins against them (Rom. 4:1-8). Sinners receive through faith in Christ alone "the gift of righteousness" (Rom 1:17; 5:17; Phil 3:9) and thus be come [*sic*] "the righteousness of God" in him who was "made sin" for them (2 Cor 5:21).

As our sins were reckoned to Christ, so Christ's righteousness is reckoned to us. This is justification by the imputation of Christ's righteousness. All we bring to the transaction is our need of it.

Faith. Our faith in the God who bestows it, the Father, the Son, and the Holy Spirit, is itself the fruit of God's grace. Faith links us savingly to Jesus, but inasmuch as it involves an acknowledgment that we have no merit of our own, it is confessedly not a meritorious work.

The Gospel assures us that all who have entrusted their lives to Jesus Christ are born-again children of God (Jn 1:12), indwelt, empowered, and assured of their status and hope by the Holy Spirit (Rom 7:6; 8:9-17). The moment we truly believe in Christ, the Father declares us righteous in him and begins conforming us to his likeness. Genuine faith acknowledges and depends upon Jesus as Lord and shows itself in growing obedience to the divine commands, though this contributes nothing to the ground of our justification (Jas 2:14-26; Heb 6:1-12).

Sanctification. By his sanctifying grace, Christ works within us through faith, renewing our fallen nature and leading us to real maturity, that measure of development which is meant by "the fullness of Christ" (Eph 4:13). The Gospel calls us to live as obedient servants of Christ and as his emissaries in the world, doing justice, loving mercy, and helping all in need, thus seeking to bear witness to the kingdom of Christ. At death, Christ takes the believer to himself (Phil 1:21) for unimaginable joy in the ceaseless worship of God (Rev 22:1-5).

Salvation. Salvation in its full sense is from the guilt of sin in the past, the power of sin in the present, and the presence of sin in the future. Thus, while in foretaste believers enjoy salvation now, they still await its fullness (Mk 14:61-62; Heb 9:28). Salvation is a Trinitarian reality, initiated by the Father, implemented by the Son, and applied by the Holy Spirit. It has a global dimension, for God's plan is to save believers out of every tribe and tongue (Rev 5:9) to be his church, a new humanity, the people of God, the body and bride of Christ, and the community of the Holy Spirit. All the heirs of final salvation are called here and now to serve their Lord and each other in love, to share in the fellowship of Jesus' sufferings, and to work together to make Christ known to the whole world.

Final judgment. We learn from the Gospel that, as all have sinned, so all who do not receive Christ will be judged according to their just deserts as measured by God's holy law, and face eternal retributive punishment.

Evangelical unity.

Unity in the gospel. Christians are commanded to love each other despite differences of race, gender, privilege, and social, political, and economic background (Jn 13:34-35; Gal 3:28-29), and to be of one mind wherever possible (Jn 17:20-21; Phil 2:2; Rom 14:1—15:13). We know that divisions among Christians hinder our witness in the world, and we desire greater mutual understanding and truth-speaking in love. We know too that as trustees of God's revealed truth we cannot embrace any form of doctrinal indifferentism, or relativism, or pluralism by which God's truth is sacrificed for a false peace.

Doctrinal disagreements call for debate. Dialogue for mutual understanding and, if possible, narrowing of the differences is valuable, doubly so when the avowed goal is unity in primary things, with liberty in secondary things, and charity in all things.

In the foregoing paragraphs, an attempt has been made to state what is primary and essential in the Gospel as evangelicals understand it. Useful dialogue, however, requires not only charity in our attitudes, but also clarity in our utterances. Our extended analysis of justification by faith alone through Christ alone reflects our belief that Gospel truth is of crucial importance and is not always well understood and correctly affirmed. For added clarity, out of love for God's truth and Christ's church, we now cast the key points of what has been said into specific affirmations and denials regarding the Gospel and our unity in it and in Christ.

The gospel revealed.

Affirmations and denials. 1. We affirm that the Gospel entrusted to the church is, in the first instance, God's Gospel (Mk 1:14; Rom 1:1). God is its author, and he reveals it to us in and by his Word. Its authority and truth rest on him alone.

We deny that the truth or authority of the Gospel derives from any human insight or invention (Gal 1:1-11). We also deny that the truth or authority of the Gospel rests on the authority of any particular church or human institution.

The power of the gospel.

Affirmations and denials. 2. We affirm that the Gospel is the saving power of God in that the Gospel effects salvation to everyone who believes, without distinction (Rom 1:16). This efficacy of the Gospel is by the power of God himself (1 Cor 1:18).

We deny that the power of the Gospel rests in the eloquence of the preacher, the technique of the evangelist, or the persuasion of rational argument (1 Cor 1:21; 2:1-5).

Man.

Affirmations and denials. 3. We affirm that the Gospel diagnoses the universal human condition as one of sinful rebellion against God, which, if unchanged, will lead each person to eternal loss under God's condemnation.

We deny any rejection of the fallenness of human nature or any assertion of the natural goodness, or divinity, of the human race.

Salvation.

Affirmations and denials. 4. We affirm that Jesus Christ is the only way of salvation, the only mediator between God and humanity (Jn 14:6; 1 Tim 2:5).

We deny that anyone is saved in any other way than by Jesus Christ and his Gospel. The Bible offers no hope that sincere worshipers of other religions will be saved without personal faith in Jesus Christ.

For the whole world.

Affirmations and denials. 5. We affirm that the church is commanded by God and is therefore under divine obligation to preach the Gospel to every living person (Lk 24:47; Mt 28:18-19).

We deny that any particular class or group of persons, whatever their ethnic or cultural identity, may be ignored or passed over in the preaching of the Gospel (1 Cor 9:19-22). God purposes a global church made up from people of every tribe, language, and nation (Rev 7:9).

Christology.

Affirmations and denials. 6. We affirm that faith in Jesus Christ as the divine Word (or Logos, Jn 1:1), the second Person of the Trinity, co-eternal and co-essential with the Father and the Holy Spirit (Heb 1:3), is foundational to faith in the Gospel.

We deny that any view of Jesus Christ which reduces or rejects his full deity is Gospel faith or will avail to salvation.

Incarnation.

Affirmations and denials. 7. We affirm that Jesus Christ is God incarnate (Jn 1:14). The virgin-born descendant of David (Rom 1:3), he had a true human nature, was subject to the Law of God (Gal 4:5), and was like us at all points, except without sin (Heb 2:17; 7:26-28). We affirm that faith in the true humanity of Christ is essential to faith in the Gospel.

We deny that anyone who rejects the humanity of Christ, his incarnation, or his sinlessness, or who maintains that these truths are not essential to the Gospel, will be saved (1 Jn 4:2-3).

Atonement.

Affirmations and denials. 8. We affirm that the Atonement of Christ by which, in his obedience, he offered a perfect sacrifice, propitiating the Father by paying for our sins and satisfying divine justice on our behalf according to God's eternal plan, is an essential element of the Gospel.

We deny that any view of the Atonement that rejects the substitutionary satisfaction of divine justice, accomplished vicariously for believers, is compatible with the teaching of the Gospel.

Obedience of Christ in life and death.

Affirmations and denials. 9. We affirm that Christ's saving work included both his life and his death on our behalf (Gal 3:13). We declare that faith in the perfect obedience of Christ by which he fulfilled all the demands of the Law of God in our behalf is essential to the Gospel.

We deny that our salvation was achieved merely or exclusively by the death of Christ without reference to his life of perfect righteousness.

Death, resurrection, ascension, session.

Affirmations and denials. 10. We affirm that the bodily resurrection of

Christ from the dead is essential to the biblical Gospel (1 Cor 15:14).

We deny the validity of any so-called gospel that denies the historical reality of the bodily resurrection of Christ.

Justification.

Affirmations and denials. 11. We affirm that the biblical doctrine of justification by faith alone in Christ alone is essential to the Gospel (Rom 3:28; 4:5; Gal 2:16).

We deny that any person can believe the biblical Gospel and at the same time reject the apostolic teaching of justification by faith alone in Christ alone. We also deny that there is more than one true Gospel (Gal 1:6-9).

Affirmations and denials. 12. We affirm that the doctrine of the imputation (reckoning or counting) both of our sins to Christ and of his righteousness to us, whereby our sins are fully forgiven and we are fully accepted, is essential to the biblical Gospel (2 Cor 5:19-21).

We deny that we are justified by the righteousness of Christ infused into us or by any righteousness that is thought to inhere within us.

Affirmations and denials. 13. We affirm that the righteousness of Christ by which we are justified is properly his own, which he achieved apart from us, in and by his perfect obedience. This righteousness is counted, reckoned, or imputed to us by the forensic (that is, legal) declaration of God, as the sole ground of our justification.

We deny that any works we perform at any stage of our existence add to the merit of Christ or earn for us any merit that contributes in any way to the ground of our justification (Gal 2:16; Eph 2:8-9; Tit 3:5).

The Spirit's indwelling.

Affirmations and denials. 14. We affirm that, while all believers are indwelt by the Holy Spirit and are in the process of being made holy and conformed to the image of Christ, those consequences of justification are not its ground. God declares us just, remits our sins, and adopts us as his children, by his grace alone, and through faith alone, because of Christ alone, while we are still sinners (Rom 4:5).

We deny that believers must be inherently righteous by virtue of their cooperation with God's life-transforming grace before God will declare them justified in Christ. We are justified while we are still sinners.

Sanctification.

Affirmations and denials. 15. We affirm that saving faith results in sanctification, the transformation of life in growing conformity to Christ through the power of the Holy Spirit. Sanctification means ongoing repentance, a life of turning from sin to serve Jesus Christ in grateful reliance on him as one's Lord and Master (Gal 5:22-25; Rom 8:4, 13-14).

We reject any view of justification which divorces it from our sanctifying union with Christ and our increasing conformity to his image through prayer, repentance, cross-bearing, and life in the Spirit.

Faith.

Affirmations and denials. 16. We affirm that saving faith includes mental assent to the content of the Gospel, acknowledgment of our own sin and need, and personal trust and reliance upon Christ and his work.

We deny that saving faith includes only mental acceptance of the Gospel, and that justification is secured by a mere outward profession of faith. We further deny that any element of saving faith is a meritorious work or earns salvation for us.

Judgment.

Affirmations and denials. 17. We affirm that, although true doctrine is vital for spiritual health and well-being, we are not saved by doctrine. Doctrine is necessary to inform us how we may be saved by Christ, but it is Christ who saves.

We deny that the doctrines of the Gospel can be rejected without harm. Denial of the Gospel brings spiritual ruin and exposes us to God's judgment.

Evangelism.

Affirmations and denials. 18. We affirm that Jesus Christ commands his followers to proclaim the Gospel to all living persons, evangelizing everyone everywhere, and discipling believers within the fellowship of the church. A full and faithful witness to Christ includes the witness of personal testimony, godly living, and acts of mercy and charity to our neighbor, without which the preaching of the Gospel appears barren.

We deny that the witness of personal testimony, godly living, and acts of mercy and charity to our neighbors constitutes evangelism apart from the proclamation of the Gospel.

Concluding salutation.

Our commitment. As evangelicals united in the Gospel, we promise to watch over and care for one another, to pray for and forgive one another, and to reach out in love and truth to God's people everywhere, for we are one family, one in the Holy Spirit, and one in Christ.

Centuries ago it was truly said that in things necessary there must be unity, in things less than necessary there must be liberty, and in all things there must be charity. We see all these Gospel truths as necessary.

Now to God, the Author of the truth and grace of this Gospel, through Jesus Christ, its subject and our Lord, be praise and glory forever and ever. Amen.

Appendix C

The Amsterdam Declaration, 2000

A Charter for Evangelism in the 21st Century

The Amsterdam Declaration is presented as a joint report of the three task groups of mission strategists, church leaders, and theologians gathered at Amsterdam 2000. It has been reviewed by hundreds of Christian leaders and evangelists from around the world. It is commended to God's people everywhere as an expression of evangelical commitment and as a resource for study, reflection, prayer, and evangelistic outreach.

Preamble

As a renewal movement within historic Christian orthodox transdenominational evangelicalism became a distinct global reality in the second half of the twentieth century [*sic*]. Evangelicals come from many churches, languages and cultures but we hold in common a shared understanding of the gospel of Jesus Christ, of the church's mission, and of the Christian commitment to evangelism. Recent documents that express this understanding include the Berlin Statement (1966), the Lausanne Covenant (1974), the Amsterdam Affirmations (1983), the Manila Manifesto (1989), and The Gospel of Jesus Christ: An Evangelical Celebration (1999). At the invitation of Dr. Billy Graham, some 10,000 evangelists, theologians, mission strategists and church leaders from more than 200 countries have assembled in Amsterdam in the year 2000 to listen, pray, worship and discern the wisdom of the Holy Spirit for the unfinished task of world evangelization. We are stirred and encouraged by the challenges we have heard and the fellowship we have shared with so many brothers and sisters in Christ. More than ever, we are resolved to make Christ known to all persons everywhere. This Amsterdam Declaration has been developed as a framework to surround the many action plans that are being made for the evangelization of the world. It is based on the principles set forth in the documents referred to above, and includes these three parts: A charter of commitments, definitions of key theological terms used in the charter, and a prayer of supplication to our Heavenly Father.

Charter of Commitments

This charter is a statement of tasks, goals and ideals for evangelism in the 21st century. The order of topics reflects the range of our concerns, not the priority of these themes.

1. ***Mission strategy and evangelism.*** The mission of the church has at its heart world evangelization. We have from our Lord a mandate to proclaim the good news of God's love and forgiveness to everyone, making disciples, baptizing, and teaching all peoples. Jesus made it clear in his last teachings that the scope of this work of evangelism demands that we give attention not only to those around us but also to the despised and neglected of society and to those at the ends of the earth. To do anything less is disobedience. In addition, we affirm the need to encourage new initiatives to reach and disciple youth and children worldwide; to make fuller use of media and technology in evangelism; and to stay involved personally in grass-roots evangelism so that our presentations of the biblical gospel are fully relevant and contextualized. We think it urgent to work toward the evangelization of every remaining unreached people group.

We pledge ourselves to work so that all persons on earth may have the opportunity to hear the gospel in a language they understand, near where they live. We further pledge to establish healthy, reproducing, indigenous churches among every people, in every place, that will seek to bring to spiritual maturity those who respond to the gospel message.

2. ***Leadership and evangelism.*** We affirm that leadership is one of Christ's gifts to the church. It does not exist for itself; it exists to lead the people of God in obedience to our Heavenly Father. Leaders must submit themselves in humility to Christ, the Head of the church, and to one another. This submission involves the acceptance of the supreme authority of scripture by which Christ rules in his church through his Spirit. The leaders' first task is to preserve the biblical integrity of the proclamation of the church and serve as vision carriers of its evangelistic vocation. They are responsible to see that vocation implemented by teaching, training, empowering and inspiring others. We must give special attention to encouraging women and young leaders in their work of evangelism. Leaders must always be careful not to block what God is doing as they exercise their strategic stewardship of the resources which Christ supplies to his body.

We pledge ourselves to seek and uphold this model of biblical servant-leadership in our churches. We who are leaders commit ourselves afresh to this pattern of leadership.

3. ***Theology and evangelism.*** Christian theology is the task of careful thinking and ordering of life in the presence of the triune God. In one sense, all Christians are theologians and must labor to be good ones rather than bad ones. This means that everyone's theology must be measured by biblical teaching from which alone we learn God's mind and will. Those called to the special vocations of evangelism, theology, and pastoral ministry must work together in the spread of the gospel throughout the world. Evangelists and pastors can help theologians maintain an evangelistic motivation, reminding them that true theology is always done in the service of the church. Theologians can help to clarify and safeguard God's revealed truth, providing resources for the training of evangelists and the grounding of new believers in the faith.

We pledge ourselves to labor constantly in learning and teaching the faith according to the Scriptures, and in seeking to ensure (1) that all who preach the gospel are theologically equipped and resourced in adequate ways for the work they have in hand, and (2) that all professional teachers of the faith share a common concern for evangelism.

4. ***Truth and evangelism.*** Under the influence of modern rationalism, secularism, and humanism (modernity), the Western intellectual establishment has largely reacted into a relativistic denial that there is any global and absolute truth (postmodernity). This is influencing popular culture throughout the world. By contrast, the gospel which is the authoritative word of the one, true and living God, comes to everyone everywhere at all times as truth in three senses: its affirmations are factually true, as opposed to false; it confronts us at every point with reality, as opposed to illusion; and it sets before us Jesus Christ, the co-Creator, Redeemer, and Lord of the world, as the Truth (that is, the one universally, real, accessible, authoritative, truth-telling, trustworthy Person), for all to acknowledge. There is a suspicion that any grand claim that there is one truth for everyone is inevitably oppressive and violent. But the gospel sets before us one who, though he was God, became man and identified with those under the bondage of sin to set them free from its enslavement. This gospel of God is both true for everyone and truly sets people free. It is therefore to be received in trust not suspicion.

We pledge ourselves to present and proclaim the biblical gospel and its Christ, always and everywhere, as fully sufficient and effective for the salvation of believers. Therefore, we oppose all skeptical and relativizing or syncretizing trends, whether rationalist or irrationalist, that treat that gospel as not fully true, and so as unable to lead believers into the new divine life that it promises them. We oppose all oppressive and destructive uses of God's wonderful truth.

5. ***Human need and evangelism.*** Both the law and the gospel uncover a lost human condition that goes beyond any feelings of pain, misery, frustration, bondage, powerlessness, and discontent with life. The Bible reveals that all human beings are constitutionally in a state of rebellion against the God who made them, and of whom they remain dimly aware; they are alienated from him, and cut off from all the enjoyment of knowing and serving him that is the true fulfillment of human nature. We humans were made to bear God's image in an endless

life of love to God and to other people, but the self-centeredness of our fallen and sinful hearts makes that impossible. Often our dishonesty leads us to use even the observance of religion to keep God at a distance, so that we can avoid having him deal with us about our ungodly self-worship. Therefore all human beings now face final condemnation by Christ the Judge, and eternal destruction, separated from the presence of the Lord.

We pledge ourselves to be faithful and compassionate in sharing with people the truth about their present spiritual state, warning them of judgment and hell that the impenitent face, and extolling the love of God who gave his Son to save us.

6. ***Religious pluralism and evangelism.*** Today's evangelist is called to proclaim the gospel in an increasingly pluralistic world. In this global village of competing faiths and many world religions, it is important that our evangelism be marked both by faithfulness to the good news of Christ and humility in our delivery of it. Because God's general revelation extends to all points of his creation, there may well be traces of truth, beauty and goodness in many non-Christian belief systems. But we have no warrant for regarding any of these as alternative gospels or separate roads to salvation. The only way to know God in peace, love and joy is through the reconciling death of Jesus Christ the risen Lord. As we share this message with others, we must do so with love and humility shunning all arrogance, hostility and disrespect. As we enter into dialogue with adherents of other religions, we must be courteous and kind. But such dialogue must not be a substitute for proclamation. Yet because all persons are made in the image of God, we must advocate religious liberty and human rights for all.

We pledge ourselves to treat those of other faiths with respect and faithfully and humbly serve the nation in which God has placed us, while affirming that Christ is the one and only Savior of the world.

7. ***Culture and evangelism.*** By the blood of the Lamb, God has purchased saints from every tribe and language and people and nation. He saves people in their own culture. World evangelization aims to see the

rise of churches that are both deeply rooted in Christ and closely related to their culture. Therefore, following the example of Jesus and Paul, those who proclaim Christ must use their freedom in Christ to become all things to all people. This means appropriate cultural identification while guarding against equating the gospel with any particular culture. Since all human cultures are shaped in part by sin, the Bible and its Christ are at key points counter-cultural to everyone of them.

We pledge ourselves to be culturally sensitive in our evangelism. We will aim to preach Christ in a way that is appropriate for the people among whom we witness and which will enrich that culture in all appropriate ways. Further, as salt and light we will seek the transforming of culture in ways that affirm gospel values.

8. ***Scripture and evangelism.*** The Bible is indispensable to true evangelism. The Word of God itself provides both the content and authority for all evangelism. Without it there is no message to preach to the lost. People must be brought to an understanding of at least some of the basic truths contained in the Scriptures before they can make a meaningful response to the gospel. Thus we must proclaim and disseminate the Holy Scriptures in the heart language of all those who we are called to evangelize and disciple.

We pledge ourselves to keep the Scriptures at the very heart of our evangelistic outreach and message, and to remove all known language and cultural barriers to a clear understanding of the gospel on the part of our hearers.

9. ***The church and evangelism.*** There is no dispute that in established congregations regular teaching for believers at all stages in their pilgrimage must be given, and appropriate pastoral care must be provided. But these concerns must not displace ongoing concern for mission, which involves treating evangelistic outreach as a continuing priority. Pastors in conjunction with other qualified persons should lead their congregations in the work of evangelism. Further, we affirm that the formation of godly, witnessing disciples is at the heart of the church's responsibility to prepare its members for their work of service. We affirm

that the church must be made a welcoming place for new believers.

We pledge ourselves to urge all congregations in and with which we serve to treat evangelism as a matter of priority at all times, and so to make it a focus of congregational praying, planning, training and funding.

10. ***Prayer and evangelism.*** God has given us the gift of prayer so that in his sovereignty he may respond in blessing and power to the cries of his children. Prayer is an essential means God has appointed for the awakening of the church and the carrying of the gospel throughout the world. From the first days of the New Testament church, God has used the fervent, persistent praying of his people to empower their witness in the Spirit, overcome opposition to the Lord's work and open the minds and hearts of those who hear the message of Christ. At special times in the history of the church, revivals and spiritual breakthroughs have been preceded by the explicit agreement and union of God's people in seasons of repentance, prayer and fasting. Today, as we seek to carry the gospel to unreached people groups in all the world, we need a deeper dependence upon God and a greater unity in prayer.

We pledge ourselves to pray faithfully for the Lord of the harvest to send out workers for his harvest field. We also pray for all those engaged in world evangelization and encourage the call to prayer in families, local churches, special assemblies, mission agencies and transdenominational ministries.

11. ***Social responsibility and evangelism.*** Although evangelism is not advocacy of any social program, it does entail social responsibility for at least two reasons. First, the gospel proclaims the kingship of the loving Creator who is committed to justice, to human life and the welfare of his creation. So evangelism will need to be accompanied by obedience to God's command to work for the good of all in a way that is fitting for the children of the Father who makes his sun shine on the evil and the good and sends his rain on the righteous and the unrighteous alike. Second, when our evangelism is linked with concern to alleviate poverty, uphold justice, oppose abuses of secular and economic power, stand against racism, and advance responsible stewardship of the global environment, it reflects the compassion of Christ and may gain an acceptance it would not otherwise receive.

We pledge ourselves to follow the way of justice in our family and social life, and to keep personal, social, and environmental values in view as we evangelize.

12. ***Holiness and evangelism.*** The servant of God must adorn the gospel through a holy life. But in recent times God's name has been greatly dishonored and the gospel discredited because of unholy living by Christians in leadership roles. Evangelists seem particularly exposed to temptations relating to money, sex, pride, power, neglect of family and lack of integrity. The church should foster structures to hold evangelists accountable for their lives, doctrine and ministries. The church should also ensure that those whose lives dishonor God and the gospel will not be permitted to serve as its evangelists. The holiness and humility of evangelists gives credibility to their ministry and leads to genuine power from God and lasting fruit.

We pledge ourselves to be accountable to the community of faith for our lives, doctrine, and ministry, to flee from sin, and to walk in holiness and humility.

13. ***Conflict, suffering and evangelism.*** The records of evangelism from the apostolic age, the state of the world around us today, and the knowledge of Satan's opposition at all times to the spread of the gospel, combine to assure us that evangelistic outreach in the twenty-first century will be an advance in the midst of opposition. Current forms of opposition, which Satan evidently exploits, include secular ideologies that see Christian faith as a hindrance to human development; political power structures that see the primacy of Christians' loyalty to their Lord as a threat to the regime; and militant expressions of non-Christian religions that are hostile to Christians for being different. We must expect, and be prepared for, many kinds of suffering as we struggle not against enemies of blood and flesh, but against the spiritual forces of evil in the heavenly places.

We pledge ourselves ever to seek to move forward wisely in personal evangelism, family evangelism, local church evangelism, and cooperative evangelism in its various forms, and to persevere in this despite the opposition we may encounter. We will stand in solidarity with our brothers and sisters in Christ who suffer persecution and even martyrdom for their faithful gospel witness.

14. Christian unity and evangelism. Jesus prayed to the Heavenly Father that his disciples would be one so that the world might believe. One of the great hindrances to evangelism worldwide is the lack of unity among Christ's people, a condition made worse when Christians compete and fight with one another rather than seeking together the mind of Christ. We cannot resolve all differences among Christians because we do not yet understand perfectly all that God has revealed to us. But in all ways that do not violate our conscience, we should pursue cooperation and partnerships with other believers in the task of evangelism practicing the well-tested rule of Christian fellowship: "In necessary things, unity; in non-essential things, liberty; in all things, charity."

We pledge ourselves to pray and work for unity in truth among all true believers in Jesus and to cooperate as fully as possible in evangelism with other brothers and sisters in Christ so that the whole church may take the whole gospel to the whole world.

DEFINITIONS OF KEY TERMS

The message we proclaim has both a propositional and an incarnational dimension—"the Word became flesh:" to deny either one is to bear false witness to Christ. Because the relation between language and reality is much debated today, it is important to state clearly what we mean by what we say. To avoid confusion and misunderstanding, then, we here define the following key words used in this Declaration. The definitions are all Trinitarian, Christocentric, and Bible-based.

1. God. The God of whom this Declaration speaks is the self-revealed Creator, Upholder, Governor and Lord of the universe. This God is eternal in his self-existence and unchanging in his holy love, goodness, justice, wisdom, and faithfulness to his promises. God in his own being is a community of three coequal and coeternal persons, who are revealed to us in the Bible as the Father, the Son, and the Holy Spirit. Together they are involved in an unvarying cooperative pattern in all God's relationships to and within this world. God is Lord of history, where he blesses his own people, overcomes and judges human and angelic rebels against his rule, and will finally renew the whole created order.

2. ***Jesus Christ.*** The Declaration takes the view of Jesus that the canonical New Testament sets forth and the historic Christian creeds and confessions attest. He was, and is, the second person of the triune Godhead, now and forever incarnate. He was virgin-born, lived a life of perfect godliness, died on the cross as the substitutionary sacrifice for our sins, was raised bodily from the dead, ascended into heaven, reigns now over the universe and will personally return for judgment and the renewal of all things. As the God-man, once crucified, now enthroned, he is the Lord and Savior who in love fulfills towards us the threefold mediational ministry of prophet, priest and king. His title, "Christ," proclaims him the anointed servant of God who fulfills all the Messianic hopes of the canonical Old Testament.

3. ***Holy Spirit.*** Shown by the words of Jesus to be the third divine person, whose name, "Spirit," pictures the energy of breath and wind, the Holy Spirit is the dynamic personal presence of the Trinity in the processes of the created world, in the communication of divine truth, in the attesting of Jesus Christ, in the new creation through him of believers and of the church, and in ongoing fellowship and service. The fullness of the ministry of the Holy Spirit in relation to the knowledge of Christ and the enjoyment of new life in him dates from the Pentecostal outpouring recorded in Acts 2. As the divine inspirer and interpreter of the Bible, the Spirit empowers God's people to set forth accurate, searching, life-transforming presentations of the gospel of Jesus Christ, and makes their communication a fruitful means of grace to their hearers. The New Testament shows us the supernatural power of the Spirit working miracles, signs and wonders, bestowing gifts of many kinds, and overcoming the power of Satan in human lives for the advancement of the gospel.

Christians agree that the power of the Holy Spirit is vitally necessary for evangelism and that openness to his ministry should mark all believers.

4. ***Bible.*** The 66 books of the Old and New Testaments constitute the written Word of God. As the inspired revelation of God in writing, the Scriptures are totally true and trustworthy, and the only infallible rule of faith and practice. In every age and every place, this authoritative Bible, by the Spirit's power, is efficacious for salvation through its witness to Jesus Christ.

5. ***Kingdom.*** The kingdom of God is his gracious rule through Jesus Christ over human lives, the course of history, and all reality. Jesus is Lord of past, present, and future, and Sovereign ruler of everything. The salvation Jesus brings and the community of faith he calls forth are signs of his kingdom's presence here and now, though we wait for its complete fulfillment when he comes again in glory. In the meantime, wherever Christ's standards of peace and justice are observed to any degree, to that degree the kingdom is anticipated, and to that extent God's ideal for human society is displayed.

6. ***Gospel.*** The gospel is the good news of the Creator's eternal plan to share his life and love with fallen human beings through the sending of his Son Jesus Christ, the one and only Savior of the world. As the power of God for salvation, the gospel centers on the life, death, resurrection and return of Jesus and leads to a life of holiness, growth in grace and hope-filled though costly discipleship in the fellowship of the church. The gospel includes the announcement of Jesus' triumph over the powers of darkness and of his supreme lordship over the universe.

7. ***Salvation.*** This word means rescue from guilt, defilement, spiritual blindness and deadness, alienation from God, and certainty of eternal punishment in hell, that is everyone's condition while under sin's dominion. This deliverance involves present justification, reconciliation to God and adoption into his family, with regeneration and the sanctifying gift of the Holy Spirit leading to works of righteousness and service here and now, and a promise of full glorification in fellowship with God in the future. This involves in the present life joy, peace, free-

dom and the transformation of character and relationships and the guarantee of complete healing at the future resurrection of the body. We are justified by faith alone and the salvation faith brings is by grace alone, through Christ alone, for the glory of God alone.

8. ***Christian.*** A Christian is a believer in God who is enabled by the Holy Spirit to submit to Jesus Christ as Lord and Savior in a personal relationship of disciple to master and to live the life of God's kingdom. The word Christian should not be equated with any particular cultural, ethnic, political, or ideological tradition or group. Those who know and love Jesus are also called Christ-followers, believers and disciples.

9. ***Church.*** The church is the people of God, the body and the bride of Christ, and the temple of the Holy Spirit. The one, universal church is a transnational, transcultural, transdenominational and multi-ethnic family of the household of faith. In the widest sense, the church includes all the redeemed of all the ages, being the one body of Christ extended throughout time as well as space. Here in the world, the church becomes visible in all local congregations that meet to do together the things that according to Scripture the church does. Christ is the head of the church. Everyone who is personally united to Christ by faith belongs to his body and by the Spirit is united with every other true believer in Jesus.

10. ***Mission.*** Formed from *missio*, the Latin word for "sending," this term is used both of the Father's sending of the Son into the world to become its Savior and of the Son's sending the church into the world to spread the gospel, perform works of love and justice, and seek to disciple everyone to himself.

11. ***Evangelism.*** Derived from the Greek word *euangelizesthai*, "to tell glad tidings," this word signifies making known the gospel of Jesus Christ so that people may trust in God through him, receiving him as their Savior and serving him as their Lord in the fellowship of his church. Evangelism involves declaring what God has done for our salvation and calling on the hearers to become disciples of Jesus through repentance from sin and personal faith in him.

12. *Evangelist.* All Christians are called to play their part in fulfilling Jesus' Great Commission, but some believers have a special call to, and a spiritual gift for, communicating Christ and leading others to him. These we call evangelists, as does the New Testament.

PRAYER

Gracious God, our Heavenly Father, we praise you for the great love that you have shown to us through the redeeming death and triumphant resurrection of your Son, our Lord Jesus Christ. We pray that you would enable us by the power of your Holy Spirit to proclaim faithfully the good news of your kingdom and your love. Forgive us for failing to take the gospel to all the peoples of the world. Deliver us from ignorance, error, lovelessness, pride, selfishness, impurity, and cowardice. Enable us to be truthful, kind, humble, sympathetic, pure, and courageous. Salvation belongs to you, O God, who sits on the throne, and to the Lamb. We ask you to make our gospel witness effective. Anoint our proclamation with the Holy Spirit; use it to gather that great multitude from all nations who will one day stand before you and the Lamb giving praise. This we ask by the merits of our Lord Jesus Christ. Amen.

Bibliography and Permissions

Amsterdam Affirmations, 1983. (Developed and released at the International Conference for Itinerant Evangelists, Amsterdam, 1983.) Evangelical Ministries to New Religions. Accessed on August 22, 2002, at <www.emnr.org/lausanne.html>. Taken from *One Race, One Gospel, One Task*, edited by Carl F. H. Henry and W. Stanley Mooneyham, Volume I, ©1967 World Wide Publications, used by permission, all rights reserved.

The Amsterdam Declaration, 2000: A Charter for Evangelism in the 21st Century. (Joint report of the three task groups of Amsterdam 2000.) Christianity Today International. Accessed on August 22, 2002, at <www.christianitytoday.com/ct/2000/132/13.0.html>. Taken from *One Race, One Gospel, One Task*, edited by Carl F. H. Henry and W. Stanley Mooneyham, Volume I, ©1967 World Wide Publications, used by permission, all rights reserved.

Arab World Ministries Doctrinal Statement. Accessed on February 7, 2003, at <www.gospelcom.net/awm/new/doctrinal_statement>. Used by permission of Arab World Ministries.

Asbury Theological Seminary Statement of Faith. Accessed on March 4, 2003, at <www.ats.wilmore.ky.us/viewpiece/vp_faith.htm>.

Azusa Pacific University Statement of Faith, 2002. Accessed on August 23, 2002, at <www.apu.edu/about/believe>. Used by permission of Azusa Pacific University.

Back to the Bible: What We Believe, 1996-2003. Excerpted from *This We Believe: Back to the Bible's Statement of Faith*, copyrighted 1987, used by permission of The Good News Broadcasting Association, Inc. All rights reserved. Accessed on February 7, 2003, at <www.backtothebible.org/aboutus/statement.htm>.

Berlin Statement, 1966 (World Congress on Evangelism, Berlin, 1966). Taken from *One Race, One Gospel, One Task*, edited by Carl F. H. Henry and

W. Stanley Mooneyham, Volume I, © 1967 World Wide Publications, used by permission, all rights reserved.

The Billy Graham Evangelistic Association Statement of Faith, 2003. Accessed on February 10, 2003, at <www.billygraham.org/aboutus/statementoffaith.asp>. Taken from *One Race, One Gospel, One Task,* edited by Carl F. H. Henry and W. Stanley Mooneyham, Volume I, ©1967 World Wide Publications, used by permission, all rights reserved.

Campus Crusade for Christ Statement of Faith, 1998. Accessed on August 23, 2002, at <www.ccci.org/faith.html>. Used by permission.

The Chicago Call: An Appeal to Evangelicals, 1977, 1998. Communion of Evangelical Episcopal Churches. Accessed on August 22, 2002, at <www.theceec.org/11chicagocall.html>. (See also Robert Webber and Donald Bloesch, eds. *The Orthodox Evangelicals*. Nashville: Nelson, 1978.) Used by permission.

The Chicago Statement on Biblical Inerrancy, 1978. (Produced by a draft committee of The International Council on Biblical Inerrancy, Chicago, 1978.) Jesus People USA. Accessed on December 10, 2000, at <www.jpusa.org/jpusa/documents/biblical.htm>. (See also *Journal of the Evangelical Theological Society* 21, no. 4 [1978]: 289-296.) Taken from *Biblical Errancy* by Norman L. Geisler. Copyright © 1981 June, by the Zondervan Corporation. Used by permission of The Zondervan Corporation.

China Graduate School of Theology Statement of Faith: Article VII of Constitution and By-Laws, 2002. Accessed on February 11, 2003, at <www.cgst.edu/US/Original/faith.html>. Used by permission of the China Graduate School of Theology.

Chosen People Ministries Doctrinal Statement, 2000, 2003. Accessed January 9, 2003, at <www.chosenpeople.com/docs/GB/About/doctrinalstatement.html>.

Christian Witness to the Jewish People, 1980. (From the Consultation on World Evangelization, Pattaya, Thailand, 1980; drafted by the Mini-Consultation on Reaching Jewish People.) Lausanne Committee for World Evangelization. Accessed on January 9, 2003, at <www.gospelcom.net/lcwe/LOP/lop07.htm>. Quoted with permission from the Lausanne Committee for World Evangelization.

Christianity Today International Statement of Faith, 1994-2000. Accessed on December 14, 2000, at <www.christianitytoday.com/help/features/faith.html>. Used by permission of Christianity Today International.

Deliver Us from Evil Consultation Statement, 2000. (Convened by the Lausanne Committee for World Evangelization and the Association of Evangelicals in Africa, Nairobi, 2000.) Lausanne Committee for World Evangelization. Accessed on January 9, 2003, at <www.gospelcom.net/lcwe/dufe/Papers/dufeeng.htm>. Quoted with permission from the Lausanne Committee for World Evangelization.

The DuPage Declaration: A Call to Biblical Fidelity. (Adopted by evangelical Renewal Executives—now The Association for Church Renewal, Wheaton, Illinois, 1990.) Brethren Revival Fellowship (BRF). Accessed on December 24, 2000, at <www.brfwitness.org/Articles/dupagedec.htm>. (See also *BRF Witness* 25, no. 5 [1990].) Printed by permission of the Association for Church Renewal.

European Christian Mission International Statement of Faith. Accessed on April 14, 2001, at <www.ecmi.org/beliefs.htm>. Quote is from "The Way Ahead" statement on doctrinal theme of church. Used by permission of European Christian Mission International.

Evangelical Association of the Caribbean Statement of Faith. E-mail from Rev. Gerry A. Seale, general secretary, to Thomas C. Oden on February 13, 2003. Used by permission of the Evangelical Association of the Caribbean.

An Evangelical Commitment to Simple Life-style, 1980. (Written and endorsed by the International Consultation on Simple Life-style, Hoddesdon, England, March, 1980; sponsored by the Lausanne Committee for World Evangelization's Theology and Education Working Group and the World Evangelical Fellowship's Theological Commission's Unit on Ethics and Society.) Lausanne Committee for World Evangelization. Accessed on February 6, 2003, at <www.gospelcom.net/lcwe/LOP/lop20.htm>. Quoted with permission from the Lausanne Committee for World Evangelization.

Evangelical Seminary of Southern Africa Statement of Faith. Accessed on June 19, 2003, at <www.essa.ac.za/faith.htm>. Used by permission of the author, Rev. Hugh Wetmore, and by the Evangelical Seminary of Southern Africa.

Evangelical Theological Society Doctrinal Basis, Article III, 2000. Accessed on February 13, 2003, at <www.etsjets.org/doctrine.html>. Used by permission of the ETS.

Evangelische Theologische Faculteit (Leuven, Belgium) Statement of Faith, 2003-2004. Accessed on November 21, 2003, at <www.bib.be/Downloads/Doctoral_Catalog03.pdf>. Used by permission of the Evangelische Theologische Faculteit, Leuven, Belgium (www.etf.edu).

Evangelism and Social Responsibility: An Evangelical Commitment, 1982. (Written during the International Consultation on the Relationship between Evangelism and Social Responsibility, Grand Rapids, Michigan, 1982; joint publication of the Lausanne Committee for World Evangelization and the World Evangelical Fellowship.) Lausanne Committee for World Evangelization. Accessed on January 9, 2003, at <www.gospelcom.net/lcwe/LOP/lop21.htm>. Quoted with permission from the Lausanne Committee for World Evangelization.

Faculté Libre de Théologie Evangélique (Vaux-sur-Seine, France) Statement of Faith (Profession de Foi). E-mail from Jacques Blocher, administrative manager, to Thomas C. Oden on December 20, 2000. Used by permission of Faculté Libre de Théologie Evangélique.

Focus on the Family Statement of Faith, 1987. Revised, 2000. Received from Focus on the Family upon request on January 22, 2001. Used by permission of Focus on the Family.

The Frankfurt Declaration on the Fundamental Crisis in Christian Mission, 1970. (Accepted by The Theological Convention, Frankfurt, Germany, 1970.) Institut Diakrisis. Accessed on July 29, 2003, at <www.institut-diakrisis.de/english.htm>. (See also *Christianity Today*, June 19, 1970, pp. 3-6.)

Fuller Theological Seminary Statement of Faith, 1972, 2003. Accessed on July 28, 2003, at <www.fuller.edu/catalog2/01_Introduction_To_Fuller/1_Ministry_of_Fuller.html>.

Fuller Theological Seminary: What We Believe and Teach, 1983, 1992, 2003. Accessed on February 13, 2003, at <www.fuller.edu/provost/aboutfuller/believe_teach.asp>.

Garden City Confession of Faith, 1921. (Taken for Statement of Christian Doctrine and Rules and Discipline of the Eastern Pennsylvania Mennonite Church and Related Areas, 1998.) Biblical Viewpoints Publications. Accessed on August 29, 2002, at <www.bibleviews.com/1921confession.html>. Used by permission.

GCM (Great Commission Ministries) Statement of Faith. Accessed on April 4,

2001, at <www.gcmweb.org/about/statement.asp>. Used by permission of Great Commission Ministries (GCM) and Great Commission Association of Churches (GCAC). GCM is the international missions agency of GCAC.

GCOWE '95 (Global Consultation on World Evangelization, Seoul, 1995) Declaration, 1998. AD 2000 & Beyond Movement. Accessed on January 9, 2003, at <www.ad2000.org/handbook/gcowedcl.htm>. Used by permission of AD 2000 & Beyond Movement.

Gordon-Conwell Theological Seminary Basis of Faith, 1996-2000. Accessed on December 9, 2000, at <www.gordonconwell.edu/admissions/catalog/intropages.pdf>. © Gordon-Conwell Theological Seminary. Reprinted by permission.

Gospel Connection International: What We Believe, 1998. Accessed on January 25, 2003, at <www.gospelconnection.com/doctrine.cfm>. Used by permission.

The Gospel of Jesus Christ: An Evangelical Celebration, 1999 by the Committee on Evangelical Unity in the Gospel. The Christian Counterculture Project. Accessed on December 9, 2000, at <www.antithesis.com/toolbox/evang_celebration.html>. (See also John N. Akers et al. *This We Believe: The Good News of Jesus Christ for the World.* Grand Rapids: Zondervan, 2000, pp. 239-48.) Used by permission.

Great Commission Manifesto, 1989. (Global Consultation for World Evangelization called by AD 2000 & Beyond, Singapore, 1989.). Accessed on January 9, 2003, at <www.ad2000.org/handbook/gcmanif.htm>. Used by permission of AD 2000 & Beyond Movement.

HCJB World Radio: What We Believe, 2002. Accessed on June 18, 2003, at <www.hcjb.org/Sections+index-req-viewarticle-artid-3-page-1.html>. Used by permission of HCJB World Radio.

IFMA (Interdenominational Foreign Mission Association) Confession of Faith. Accessed on April 4, 2001, at <www.ifmamissions.org/doctrin.htm>. Used by permission of IFMA.

The Iguassu Affirmation, 1999. (Emerged from the Iguassu Missiological Consultation, convened by the World Evangelical Fellowship Missions Commission, Foz do Iguassu, Brazil, 1999.) Presbyterian Frontier Fellowship. Accessed July 24, 2002, at <www.pff.net/Resources/iguassuaffirmation.htm>. (See also William D. Tayler, ed. *Global Missiology for the 21st Century: The*

Iguassu Dialogue. Grand Rapids: Baker Academic, 2000, pp. 15-21.) Used by permission of World Evangelical Alliance.

International Pentecostal Church of Christ Statement of Faith. Accessed January 7, 2003, at <http://members.aol.com/hqipcc/doctrine.html>. Permission granted by the International Pentecostal Church of Christ.

InterVarsity Christian Fellowship/USA Doctrinal Basis. Accessed on July 28, 2003, at <www.intervarsity.org/aboutus/doctrine.php>. ©2000 by InterVarsity Christian Fellowship/USA. Used by permission.

Japan Bible Seminary Doctrinal Statement. E-mail from Kazuhiko Uchida, dean, to Thomas C. Oden on December 11, 2000. Used by permission of Japan Bible Seminary.

Jews for Jesus Statement of Faith, 2001. Accessed on April 4, 2001, at <www.jfjonline.org/about/statementoffaith.htm>.

Lausanne Covenant, 1974. (International Congress on World Evangelization, Lausanne, Switzerland, 1974.) Accessed on December 8, 2000, at <www.gospelcom.net/lcwe/statements/covenant.html>. Quoted with permission from the Lausanne Committee for World Evangelization.

Liebenzell Mission of USA Statement of Faith, 2003. Accessed on July 28, 2003, at <www.liebenzellusa.org/aboutLM_USA.htm#What%20We%20Believe%20.%20.%20>. Used by permission of Liebenzell Mission of USA, Inc.

"Living Word for a Dying World" Common Commitment, 1994. Extract from the statement, "A Common Commitment," adopted by the participants of a Consultation, "Living Word for a Dying World," called and organized by the International Forum of Bible Agencies, 20-25 April, 1994. Lausanne Committee for World Evangelization. Accessed on January 10, 2003, at <www.gospelcom.net/lcwe/statements/living.html>. Used by permission.

London Bible College Doctrinal Basis. Accessed on June 19, 2003, at <www.londonbiblecollege.ac.uk/us/who-we-are/basis.shtml>. Extracted from the Doctrinal Basis of London Bible College. Used by permission of London Bible College.

Manila Manifesto, 1989. (Accepted by the Second International Congress on World Evangelization/Lausanne II, Manila, Philippines, 1989.) Lausanne Committee for World Evangelization. Accessed on December 23, 2000, at <www.gospelcom.net/lcwe/statements/manila.html>. Quoted with permission from the Lausanne Committee for World Evangelization.

A Mennonite Confession of Faith, 1990. (Formulated by The Fellowship of Concerned Mennonites.) Biblical Viewpoints Publications. Accessed on August 29, 2002, at <www.bibleviews.com/FCMstate.html>. Used by permission of The Fellowship of Concerned Mennonites.

The National Association of Evangelicals: An Evangelical Manifesto, 1996, 2002. Accessed on February 26, 2003, at <www.nae.net/index.cfm/method/content.8817C848-14ED-4E90-813D534F81EAEEBF>.

The National Association of Evangelicals Statement of Faith, 2002. Accessed on November 22, 2003, at <www.nae.net/index.cfm/method/index.cfm?FUSEACTION=nae.statement_of_faith>.

Network of International Christian Schools Statement of Faith, 2002. Accessed on February 7, 2003, at <www.nics.org/statement.html>. Used by permission of the Network of International Christian Schools, Inc.

North American Indian Ministries (NAIM) Doctrinal Statement, 2000. Accessed on April 4, 2001, at <www.naim.ca/doctrinalstatement.php>. Used by permission of NAIM.

OMS International Statement of Faith, 2002. Accessed on January 10, 2003, at <www.omsinternational.org>. Used by permission.

Pentecostal/Charismatic Churches of North America (previously Pentecostal Fellowship of North America) Statement of Faith, 1994. Revised, 1998, 2002. Accessed on January 10, 2003, at <www.pctii.org/pccna/art3.html>.

Prison Fellowship Ministries Statement of Faith, 2002. Accessed on November 22, 2003, at <www.pfm.org>. Reprinted with permission from the Prison Fellowship Ministries Statement of Faith (www.prisonfellowship.org).

Regent University Philosophy of Education, 2003. Accessed on November 22, 2003, at <http://web.regent.edu/acad/schdiv/assets/admissions/docs/community%20life.pdf>. Courtesy of Regent University.

Society for Pentecostal Studies Bylaws, 1979 (adopted from the Statement of Purpose of the World Pentecostal Fellowship), 2000-2002. Accessed on January 14, 2003, at <www.sps-usa.org/about/mission.html>. Used by permission of Society for Pentecostal Studies.

South America Mission Doctrinal Statement. Accessed on April 4, 2001, at <www.samlink.org/pages/DoctrinalStatement.htm>. Used by permission of South America Mission.

South Asia Institute of Advanced Christian Studies Statement of Faith. E-mail from Dr. Graham Houghton, principal, to Thomas C. Oden on March 13, 2003. Taken from the statement of faith of the South Asia Institute of Advanced Christian Studies (SAIACS), Bangalore, India.

Transformation: The Church in Response to Human Need, 1983. (Outgrowth of the Consultation on The Church in Response to Human Need, sponsored by the World Evangelical Fellowship, Wheaton, Illinois.) Lausanne Committee for World Evangelization. Accessed on January 9, 2003, at <www.gospelcom.net/lcwe/statements/wheaton83.htm>. In *The Church in Response to Human Need.* Edited by Vinay Samuel and Chris Sugden. Grand Rapids: Eerdmans, 1987; Eugene, Ore.: Wipf and Stock, 2003. Reprinted in *Mission as Transformation.* Edited by Vinay Samuel and Chris Sugden. Oxford: Regnum, 1999. Used by permission.

Trinity International University Statement of Faith, 2000-2003. Statement of faith for Trinity International University and the Evangelical Free Church of America. Accessed on February 27, 2003, at <www.tiu.edu/catalogs/divinity2002/teds_cat_01f_ doctrine.htm>. Used by permission.

Tyndale University College & Seminary Faith Statement, 2003. Accessed on February 27, 2003, at <www.tyndale.ca/about/mission.php>. Used by permission of Tyndale University College & Seminary.

Universities and Colleges Christian Fellowship (UCCF—UK) Doctrinal Basis, 1995, 2003. Accessed on February 27, 2003, at <www.uccf.org.uk/resources/db/index.php>. Used by permission of UCCF.

Wheaton College Statement of Faith, 2003. Accessed on February 7, 2003, at <www.wheaton.edu/welcome/mission.html>. Used by permission of Wheaton College.

The Willowbank Declaration on the Christian Gospel and the Jewish People, 1989. (Developed and adopted at the Willowbank Consultation on the Gospel and the Jewish People, 1989; sponsored by the World Evangelical Fellowship and supported by the Lausanne Committee.) World Evangelical Alliance. Accessed on January 10, 2003, at <www.worldevangelical.org/willowbank_19sep02.doc>. Used by permission of World Evangelical Alliance.

Word in Action (Bath Convention—Keswick Convention) Basis of Faith. Accessed on January 14, 2003, at <www.wordinaction.supanet.com>.

World Evangelical Alliance (WEA) Statement of Faith, 2001. Accessed on February 13, 2003, at <www.worldevangelical.org/textonly/3statefaith.htm>.

Used by permission of World Evangelical Alliance.

World Gospel Mission Statement of Faith, 1997-2002. Accessed on January 9, 2003, at <www.wgm.org/cms/AboutUs/Default.asp?did=219&pid=236>. Used with permission of World Gospel Mission.

World Vision Statement of Faith, 2003. Accessed on November 22, 2003, at <www.worldvision.org/worldvision/hr.nsf/stable/HR_faith#faith>.

Scripture Index